HANDBOOK FOR NONVIOLENT CAMPAIGNS

PUBLISHED BY WAR RESISTERS' INTERNATIONAL
FEBRUARY 2009

ISBN 978-0-903517-21-8

CREDITS

The process of writing this Handbook was a collective effort, with different layers of involvement. An international editorial committee did most of the editorial work. The articles were worked out on the WRI Wiki (http://wri-irg.org/wiki/index.php/Nonviolence_Handbook); the contents in the Wiki will continue to be updated.

Coordination
Howard Clark
Javier Gárate
Joanne Sheehan

Editorial Committee
Howard Clark
Javier Gárate
Joanne Sheehan
Dorie Wilsnack

Copyediting
Shannon McManimon

Layout
FEMØNIC

Graphics
Boro Kitanoski

Contributors
Eric Bachman, Roberta Bacic, Jungmin Choi, Ruben Dario Santamaria, Ippy, Hilal Demir, Ruth Hiller, Jørgen Johansen, Brian Martin, Martin Smedjeback, Andreas Speck, Majken Sorensen, Roel Stynen, Ferda Ülker, Stellan Vinthagen

Reviewers
Thank you to the following reviewers who helped in the process of producing the Handbook:
Hans Lammerant, Tali Lerner, Vicki Rover, Chesterfield Samba, Christine Schweitzer, Vivien Sharples, Jill Sternberg,

CONTENTS

1

ABOUT THIS HANDBOOK
AND HOW TO USE IT

War Resisters' International (WRI) produced this Handbook, drawing on the experiences of groups in many countries and different generations of activists. At the heart of every nonviolent campaign are the resourcefulness and commitment of the activists involved and the quality of the message with which they reach out — a message that may raise questions about how things are, stir people out of resignation about what is happening or might happen, attract allies, or demand a say in decisions that affect their/our lives. One of the notions central to nonviolent campaigns is 'empowerment': a sense of how you can make things happen, especially if you join with others.

There are many dramatic images of nonviolent action. Indeed, the ability to dramatise an issue is one of the strengths of nonviolence; it tries to make people see and act on what often passes unnoticed. However, this drama doesn't just happen. It gestates — in groups or cells of activists, in discussions, in training sessions, in reflecting on previous experiences, in planning, in experimenting, in making contacts. That is why this Handbook is grounded in what groups have done and how they have done it. We are not attempting to present a definitive model, but to suggest methods that have worked in various contexts and that can be adapted by creative nonviolent activists in their own situations.

Thus, this printed Handbook is a selection of a wider range of material available from War Resisters' International or on the internet. It combines texts introducing certain themes, experiences, and group exercises. The introductory section outlines what we mean by nonviolence; the importance of nonviolence training; issues for your group; and a few brief examples of historical nonviolence. Section Three looks at one specific instance of oppression within our movements: gender. Section Four outlines tasks and tools for organising and facilitating trainings. Section Five describes nonviolent campaigns and actions, including constructive programmes and the role of the media. Section Six offers specific tips for effective organising at all stages. Section Seven provides stories and strategies from around the world.

Throughout the Handbook we describe some of the advantages of nonviolence in action and give examples of how it works. If you are unfamiliar with terms in the Handbook, see the glossary (Section Ten, p143).

Section Eight gives examples of exercises for working in nonviolence. These group exercises aim either to deepen a group's understanding of an issue and of each other or to help the group be more effective in carrying out nonviolent actions and campaigns. In general, the exercises need somebody to 'facilitate' them, that is to introduce them, explain what to do and why, and keep the process moving, encouraging timid people to speak up and extroverts to listen, especially in the 'debriefing' at the end. Notes about exercises are marked with the ⇨ symbol.

We hope that readers will copy parts of this Handbook and translate them or hand out to their groups. If you do this, feel free to adapt what is written to suit your needs. Section Nine offers advice — and therefore encouragement! — for you to tailor what you find here or on the WRI Website to your own situation.

Section Eleven contains selected resources. If you find something in this Handbook particularly interesting, you can also go to the WRI Website (http://wri-irg.org/wiki/index.php/Nonviolence_Handbook) to find out more. You will find longer versions of some articles, additional articles and exercises, and plenty more resources. In WRI we try to share rather than provide resources, meaning that others would love to read what you have learnt in your experiences with nonviolent campaigns or training. So please contribute to the WRI Website. And if you do translate part of the Handbook, please send your translation to info@wri-irg.org so we can add it to the Website.

2

INTRODUCTION TO NONVIOLENCE

What is Nonviolence and Why Use It?

Why are you interested in a Handbook on nonviolent campaigns? Probably because you want to make something happen, or perhaps because you want to stop something from happening. Perhaps you sense that nonviolence can offer an alternative to actions that generate hostility and ultimately prove sterile, at least from the point of view of making social change. Perhaps you just want to try something different or get some tips to improve the way your group is already organising actions and campaigns.

In this Handbook, our basic, working definition of nonviolence is based on a desire to end violence — be it physical violence or what's been called 'structural violence' (deprivation, social exclusion, and oppression) — without committing further violence. This is not a definitive description, as other, more eloquent, more philosophical, more time-specific (e.g., that meant a lot in a certain time and place), and personal, rather poetic, definitions exist.

Nonviolence can imply much more than this basic definition, including a desire to change power relations and social structures, an attitude of respect for all humanity or all life, or even a philosophy of life or theory of social action. We encourage you to explore these areas. Discovering the differences in emphasis and sharing insights into nonviolence can be a rich experience in the context of a group preparing to take nonviolent action together.

People have different reasons for adopting nonviolence. Some advocate it because they see it as an effective technique for bringing about desired social changes, others because they seek to practise nonviolence as a way of life. There is a spectrum here, with many somewhere in between. Such differences may surface during a campaign, but usually a statement of principles or guidelines specific to a particular campaign (see 'Principles of Nonviolent Action' p31 and 'Nonviolent Guidelines' p32) can accommodate people with attitudes across this spectrum.

Certain differences in understanding, however, can be a source of friction in a campaign and need to be brought into the open. For instance, some argue that the methods of nonviolence should be deployed in order to wage a conflict and win; others argue that a key nonviolent attitude is to seek a solution that

ACTION AT MILITARY BARRACKS IN BILBAO, BASQUE COUNTRY, DURING THE 2006 FOOTBALL WORLD CUP.
PHOTO: KEM-MOC

will include those who today are adversaries. What is essential when a difference such as this occurs is not that campaigners debate basic attitudes, but that they reach agreements on the points that affect the campaign. This particular example (when some seek to 'win' and others seek an inclusive solution) would influence the demands and negotiating strategy the activists engaging in the campaign draw up.

The question of damage to property can be divisive. Some nonviolent activists seek to avoid damage to property while others believe that damaging property is a cost worth inflicting on an opponent. In Section Five, we discuss the value of campaign or action guidelines. Attitudes on a subject like property damage might need to be debated in drawing up such guidelines. Such discussion should not be delayed until an action is underway. For some people, nonviolent action means avoiding hostile behaviour towards adversaries, perhaps even 'seeking that of good in everyone', while other nonviolent activists might seek to 'shame' an adversary, or to brand them as 'war criminals' or 'torturers', 'racists', or 'corrupt'. The issue of shouting names or terms of abuse might well be covered in the guidelines for an action, but the underlying differences and the possible combinations of attitudes can be discussed in much greater depth by the kind of 'affinity groups' discussed in the section on preparing for nonviolent action (see 'Affinity Groups', p71). Such groups aim to be a 'safe space' for disclosing doubts, but also for mutual learning. Affinity group members can take a phrase commonly associated with nonviolent action

— such as 'speaking truth to power' — and each explain what it means for her or him and what issues it raises, sharing insights and deepening each other's understanding of what they are trying to do together.

A common attitude of nonviolent activists is that we want our activities to be an expression of the future we are trying to create: this might be embodied in what Mohandas Gandhi called constructive programme (see "Constructive Programme', p40), but also in the idea of we/the movement 'being peace', that our behaviour reflects the world we want. When we use phrases such as 'speaking truth to power', 'affirming life', or 'respecting diversity', we are invoking fundamental values that themselves are a source of strength for us and a point of contact with those we want to reach.

"My first training experience was for the 15th of May action in Israel in 2003. I was a Chilean conscientious objector who had been involved in campaigning against militarism for a number of years. The training was truly empowering to me, and I went back home with the urge to share what I had learned and that if we wanted to be successful in our actions, training ourselves was going to be essential. The next actions we did were not just with all the group standing in front of the military building but with a higher level of risk because of the higher level of confidence we had, because we were prepare and trained for it."

Javier Gárate

How Does Nonviolence Work?

Nonviolence strengthens a campaign in three ways:

1. Among participants in a campaign. In fostering trust and solidarity among participants, they (ideally) are put in touch with the sources of their own power to act in the situation. Many people don't realise how creative they can be until they have support of others in trying something new.
2. In relation to a campaign's adversary. Nonviolence aims either to inhibit the violence of an adversary or to ensure that violent repression will 'backfire' politically against them. Beyond that, it seeks to undermine an oppressive institution's 'pillars of power' (see 'Pillars of Power' or 'Spectrum of Allies' Exercises, p128). Rather than treating employees of our opponents as inani mate tools, nonviolence tries to create possibilities for them to rethink their allegiances.
3. In relation to others not yet involved. Nonviolence changes the quality of communication with bystanders or 'outsiders' — people not yet concerned about the issue or not yet active about it, people who can be potential allies

 See 'Spectrum of Allies' Exercise, p130.

NONVIOLENT DIRECT ACTION TRAINING IN SANTIAGO, CHILE.　　　PHOTO: ANDREAS SPECK

The pioneer of nonviolent scholarship was Gene Sharp, who has suggested four mechanisms of change in those opposing a nonviolent struggle:

a) conversion: occasionally a campaign will persuade them to its point of view;
b) coercion: sometimes a campaign can coerce adversaries to back down without convincing them of the activists' views of right and wrong;
c) accommodation: when an adversary looks for some way to 'accommodate' a campaign, to make a concession without granting everything a campaign demands and without relinquishing power;
d) disintegration: a mechanism Sharp added after 1989 when Soviet-aligned regimes had lost so much legitimacy and had so little capacity to renew themselves that, in the face of a 'people power' challenge, they disintegrated.

* *For more, see 'Forms of Action', p46.*

Scholarship on nonviolence tends to look more at the ultimate success of a movement, in particular the leverage it succeeded in exerting on those in power. This Handbook, however, is more concerned with looking at processes involved in building campaigns, in making issues alive and tangible, in designing campaign strategies, and in preparing and evaluating action. What we write is firmly grounded in the practice of social movements, and in particular our own experiences with the peace, antimilitarist, anti-nuclear, and social justice movements of various countries.

Nonviolence Training

We don't say that you need nonviolence training before you go out on the street and hold up a placard or give out a leaflet. Not in most countries anyway. However, the whole process we refer to as nonviolence training — analysing issues, envisioning alternatives, drawing up demands, developing campaign strategy, planning actions, preparing actions, evaluating actions or campaigns — can increase the impact your group has on others, help you to function better in action and cope better with the risks and problems it poses, and expand your action horizons. Basically, nonviolence training helps to create a safe space to test out and develop new ideas or to analyse and evaluate experiences.

Nonviolence training can help participants form a common understanding of the use of nonviolence in campaigns and actions. It is a participatory educational experience where we can learn new skills and unlearn destructive and oppressive behaviours society has taught us. Nonviolence training can strengthen a group, developing a community bond while people learn to work better together and clarify their intentions. Nonviolence training can help us understand and develop the power of nonviolence. It gives an opportunity to share concerns, fears, and feelings and to discuss the role of oppression in our society and our groups. Individually, training helps build self-confidence and clarify our personal interactions. The goal of nonviolence training is empowering the participants to engage more effectively in collective action. The process includes various exercises and training methods, some of which are included in this Handbook in Section Eight.

Nonviolence training can prepare people for participation in nonviolent direct action, teach strategy development techniques and the skills needed to engage in the strategy, and work on group process and issues of oppression. Nonviolence trainings are often used to prepare people for specific actions, to learn about the scenario, to develop a plan and practice it, to understand the legal issues, and more. They are an opportunity for a group to build solidarity and to develop affinity groups. Through role playing (see 'Role Playing' Exercise, p134), people can learn what they might expect from police, officials, other people in the action, and themselves. It can help people decide if they are prepared to participate in the action.

Nonviolence trainings can range from several hours to several months, depending on factors such as the campaign's needs and timeline, the goals for the training, and the experience and availability of the participants and trainers.

✱ *See 'Tasks and Tools for Organising and Facilitating Trainings', p27, for more on planning nonviolence trainings.*

Role of Trainers

A nonviolence trainer is someone who can facilitate a group through a learning process. A trainer must be knowledgeable regarding the topics of the training, but should not be a know-it-all. A trainer's goal is to guide the participants to develop their own ideas, not to tell people what to think and do.

We realise that not all groups and communities who want nonviolence training have local trainers. But when people understand what skills are needed to conduct a training, they may realise they have already developed some of those skills and used them in different contexts. You can create a training team of co-facilitators who together can bring their skills and experience. If possible, the training team should reflect the participants, consisting of women and men and people of various ages and ethnic backgrounds.

Trainers need

■ Good group process skills and an awareness of group dynamics. It is the role of the trainer to make sure everyone participates and feels able to share insights and experiences.

■ An understanding of nonviolent actions and campaigns. If no one has experience, the trainer needs to use case studies and exercises to help the group learn.

■ To learn how and when to use the right exercises, being sensitive to the needs and styles of groups.

Potential Topics for Nonviolence Training

■ History and philosophy of nonviolence and practice of nonviolent action.

■ Overcoming oppression, ethnic/racial, and gender dynamics (See Section Three and Resources in Section Eleven).

■ Campaign strategy development (see Section Five).

■ Consensus decision-making and quick decision-making (see 'Working in Groups', p71, and 'Decision-Making' Exercise, p133).

■ What an affinity group is and roles within the group (see 'Affinity Groups', p71, and 'Roles In, Before, and After an Action, p86).

■ Skills such as legal and media work (see 'Legal Support', p87, and 'The Role of Media', p49).

You and Your Group

This Handbook is written for groups, perhaps a group that has come together for a specific cause or with a specific theme, perhaps a group based on friendship or affinity in what you feel about the world, perhaps even a group formed for one occasion. Even an individual stand usually requires on some group support. The campaigns section of the Handbook (Section Five) is more useful for groups who plan to stay together for the long-term, while the section on preparing for action (Section Four) might be more appropriate for those joining together for a specific event.

Strong groups of people who stay together, who work well together and strengthen each other, give a movement strength. Groups come together in many different ways, and those that are most effective and enjoyable tend to have something distinctive, some mark of their own creativity, some characteristic that makes them flourish. This arises from the special combinations that happen within a group and the particular balance the group arrives at between the various desires and talents of its members.

This section offers some perspectives that you might think about as a member of the group, some of which the group will discuss and make a conscious decision on, some of which will evolve.

Strengthening a Group

The first point is how much importance people attach to the way the group itself functions and its attitudes. This itself can be a never-ending source of conflict! There are balances to be struck, such as between those impatient with discussion who urgently want to be out 'there' and 'doing', and those who want more clarity, be it about goals, about being prepared to argue a case in public, about who the group should try to reach and the forms of action it should consider, or about how the group organises itself and functions. Somehow a new group has to do its best to find its own way and overall direction, some happy medium between people pulling in different directions. If the group has a lot of energy and initiative, sub-groups may take up particular themes. If the group involves people with conflicting political philosophies or attitudes, that needs to be acknowledged and made a source of strength rather than a block on creativity.

Whether your group is large and open or small and limited by affinity (see 'Affinity Groups', p71) you want new people to feel welcome, and you want everyone to feel able to contribute. This raises issues of cultural diversity, of oppressive behaviour, of class, race and gender dynamics, and of power within the group. Dealing with these issues can itself be a source of tension, although not dealing with them can be even worse. You'll need to find ways to tackle these questions in a supportive atmosphere. Section Three on gender offers some examples.

In general, it is useful for a group that plans to stay together to organise some special sessions in addition to the usual meetings, or to set aside a slot in

15

the regular meetings for something a bit different. At times, this might have a practical focus, such as skill-sharing, campaign development, or even a more detailed look at a particular campaign topic. At times, this might be more group-directed, such as activities that build rapport (banner-making, singing) or ways to improve group functioning.

Exploring Differences

A nonviolent action group will also at some point benefit from considering some of the issues attached to the term nonviolence — including forms of nonviolence and their repercussions, values, attitudes, and goals. Any issue that touches on group members' deeply held convictions must be handled with respect for differences, aiming less to establish a group position than to share perceptions and perspectives. Simply understanding each other better will deepen what you're trying to do together.

Take the question of nonviolence itself. A commitment to nonviolence can be a unifying factor for a group, but is not necessarily so; there are often divisions, especially between those prepared to use nonviolence for specific purposes and those who hold it as a far-reaching philosophy. We suggest that some issues might be dealt with by a collective declaration of principles (see 'Principles of Nonviolent Action', p31, and 'Nonviolence Guidelines', p32), but even a group that expresses a commitment to nonviolent action will have different preconceptions about other aspects, both positive and negative of nonviolence. A good discussion around the issues might be stimulating, even inspiring, but a not-so-good one can exacerbate tensions and frustration.

A relatively safe way of exploring differences is a 'barometer' of values, also known as a 'spectrum' exercise. Someone develops a set of questions to explore different attitudes, actions, and factors. The questions are posed to the group, and people move on two axes: one, it is or isn't nonviolent, and two, I would or wouldn't do it myself. This can later develop into 'I would or would not want to be part of a group doing this'.

 See 'Spectrum/Barometer' Exercise, p140.

A question like 'what is your group trying to achieve'? can have one simple answer, but each person in the group may have additional goals. Many different lines of thought or feeling can lead people to be involved in a group. Something as simple as a paired introductions exercise can be a good start in giving people space to explain what brought them.

In general, this Handbook does not much explore the perspective from which you engage in action, beyond a fairly loose idea of social transformation. Such perspectives will vary greatly from group to group and in different contexts. The point is not to establish uniformity, but to understand and even appreciate people's different ways of looking at things. In particular, if your group is considering something risky, you need to take the time to prepare properly, understanding the distinct attitudes each of you brings to the action and your preferences for how to respond to the risk.

How you understand the context in which you act affects your choice of methods. Commentators sometimes distinguish between 'conventional' and 'unconventional' forms of action. However, context can change all that. In a closed society, simply 'saying the unsayable' or 'breaking the silence' by quite conventional means can have an enormous, perhaps explosive, perhaps catalytic, impact. However, in other contexts, 'non-conventional' action — such as civil disobedience or strikes — might have become contained or normalised. Either because non-participants ignore it as 'oh, it's just them doing their thing again', or because the participants themselves have gotten stuck in a routinised form of action. Some social movement theorists (see Doug McAdam, Sidney Tarrow, and Charles Tilly, Dynamics of Contention, Cambridge University Press, 2001, pp7-9) have suggested that 'transgressive' and 'contained' action is a more useful distinction than 'conventional'/'non-conventional' action because it acknowledges the different impact various forms of action can have in different contexts. Some of the differences within your group (for instance, in attitudes to illegal activity) might stem from different analyses of the context for your action.

✱ For more on contexts, see 'Sending the Protest Message', p57, and 'Coping with the Stress and Strain of Taking a Stand', p63.

What Do You Want?

As an activist, you need to think about what you want from a group. Do you want a group that attracts a wide range of people? Do you want a group with people who share a lot of attitudes and convictions and that will make a strong statement of those? Is there a way of combining the two? For instance, could you be part of an affinity group promoting nonviolence in the context of a broader campaign?

Until your group starts to take action, you don't know how much impact you could have. Groups usually don't sense the possibilities they can open until they actually go public. Just 14 women took part in the first demonstration of Las Madres de la Plaza de Mayo in Buenos Aires; some other powerful movements began even smaller. Some simple, small actions have had far greater consequences than anyone could imagine. However, you also have to recognise that plenty of actions have much smaller consequences. A nonviolent action group needs to be aware of its full repertoire of action, have a strong sense of purpose, and be capable of analysing the context it is working in. This Handbook therefore includes material about preparing for action, about building up a campaign and about evaluating what you've done.

Historical Uses of Nonviolence

Look at the history of your country and you will find episodes of nonviolent action: demonstrations, strikes, boycotts, or other forms of popular non-cooperation. The causes will vary — for the rights of workers and peasants, freedom for slaves, the right to vote for women or people without property, for racial equality, for gender equality, for freedom from occupation. In short, the causes encompass a range of forms of injustice and domination. However, not until the twentieth century — and in particular the campaigns of Mohandas Gandhi in South Africa and India — did movements discuss nonviolent action as a conscious strategy for social transformation.

Gandhi was convinced that nonviolence had a particular power, both in its effect on the people who undertook action and on those at whom the action was directed. He saw that social solidarity can overcome efforts to dominate, exploit, or otherwise oppress a population. He also believed that it was not enough just to oppose an adversary, blaming them for everything, but that people must look at their own responsibilities and behaviour. Freedom and justice are not just to be demanded but to be practised and to be the basis on which a movement constructs itself. Gandhi wrote streams of articles developing his ideas about nonviolence. He was not the first to observe that those who rule depend on the cooperation of those they rule, but he made this central to his strategies of civil resistance: 'the first principle of nonviolence', he once wrote, 'is non-cooperation with everything humiliating'. Gandhi was not the most systematic thinker about nonviolence — he preferred to talk about his experience as 'experiments with Truth' — but he insisted on certain fundamentals. One was the need for campaigns to maintain a nonviolent discipline. Another was the central importance of constructive activity addressing problems among the population (for more, see 'Constructive Programme', p40). For Gandhi in the context of colonised India, this constructive programme expanded to include reducing inter-religious hostility, tackling discrimination along gender or caste lines, countering illiteracy and ignorance on sanitation, and promoting self-sufficiency in food and clothing production.

Most participants in the campaigns Gandhi initiated shared only some of his principles; they were prepared to use nonviolence to free India from British colonialism, but few had Gandhi's utter commitment to nonviolence as a way of life. Indeed, most conventional political leaders gave only symbolic importance to the constructive programme. This pattern has frequently been repeated: nonviolent action has been effective when used by broad movements where most participants accept nonviolence in practical terms as the appropriate strategy for their situation but only a minority express a philosophical commitment. The example of the Indian independence struggle had a huge influence on subsequent movements against colonialism, especially in Africa; people in a wide range of contexts began to study what makes nonviolence effective and how it can be used even more successfully. Sixty years after Gandhi's death, nonviolent activists are still 'experimenting with truth', and a field studying what makes nonviolence effective has grown.

What Works Where

The style of nonviolence varies a lot according to context. Since the term 'people power' was coined when the Marcos regime in the Philippines was brought down in 1986, and especially since the downfall of Miloševic in Serbia in 2000, some observers have talked of an 'action template', meaning popular nonviolent action overthrowing a corrupt and authoritarian regime that was attempting to win elections by fraud. Of course, there are similarities between the downfall of Miloševic and 'people power' episodes elsewhere. Indeed, some of the Serbs who used nonviolence so creatively against Miloševic have now become involved in training other movements. However, in each situation, the movements have to do their own analysis of what is appropriate and what will work.

Many people are sceptical about the power of nonviolence against entrenched and brutal regimes. In such situations any resistance is likely to be difficult. Nonviolence does not offer a 'quick fix' in these situations — and neither does armed struggle. Some idealistic movements have turned to armed struggle only to find themselves increasingly separated from the population, depending on extortion and kidnapping to maintain themselves, and in short, degenerating into armed bands. Nonviolence aims to work differently. By expanding the social spaces that a movement can occupy, and by giving voice to what the regime requires should not be said, processes of fundamental change can be set in motion. Nonviolent action in the face of torture, 'disappearances', and death squads in various parts of Latin America in the 1970s and 1980s aimed to rebuild a social solidarity that could overcome fear.

In the former Soviet bloc, many were cautious about resistance, not wishing to provoke repression or Soviet military intervention. In 1970, four strikers in Gdansk, Poland, were shot dead; so when Solidarnosc was formed in 1980, Gdansk strikers avoided street confrontations, locking themselves inside their shipyard instead. They aspired to a different society, but now limited their demands to an essential first step: the recognition of free trade unions. It was a limited objective behind which all Polish workers could unite. Polish intellectuals described this as 'the self-limiting revolution'. Despite such caution, Solidarnosc's mobilising power scared the regime into imposing martial law and imprisoning many activists. But within a few years, the time came to go beyond these self-imposed limits, to make other demands, and to risk more provocative forms of nonviolent action, not just in Poland but throughout the Soviet bloc.

Most readers of this Handbook live in societies that have more 'freedom of speech' than under Soviet Communism or Latin American military dictatorships, but where activists complain of social 'apathy' that occurs as the public is bombarded with images trying to get us to buy more. Violence in our societies is most likely to be hidden away or accepted as 'the status quo', the way things are; it includes the many forms of state violence right up to weapons of mass destruction, the violence of social deprivation and environmental devastation, and the violence of remote puppetmasters pulling strings across the globe.

In these situations, social movements have a wide choice of actions, and boundaries that are continually changing — actions that broke new ground yesterday have become merely routine today. Even the disruptive has become contained.

The Role of Pacifists

We in the WRI embrace nonviolence as a matter of principle. We recognise that this commitment makes us a minority and requires us to work with people who do not necessarily share our pacifist principles. We want to look beyond rhetoric or short-term shock tactics to develop forms of active nonviolence that challenge systems of oppression and seek to construct alternatives. This means defining goals that make sense to a spectrum of people broader than just pacifists or antimilitarists as well as using methods and forms of organisation that are attractive to people who do not necessarily have a pacifist philosophy.

Because pacifists refuse to resort to violence to achieve our goals, we need to invest our creative energy in trying to develop nonviolent alternatives. Historically, pacifists have played a vital, innovative role in social movements, developing nonviolent methods of action both at the level of tactics and in forms of organising. For instance, the first U.S. 'freedom rides' against racial segregation in the 1940s were a pacifist initiative, as was the British nonviolent direct action against weapons in the 1950s. The creative use of nonviolence of these groups opened spaces for a much more widespread use of nonviolence by the mass movements that followed. Later came the introduction of nonviolence training, initially preparing people for the kind of violence that they might meet in nonviolent protests. Subsequently nonviolence training has played an essential role in promoting more participatory forms of movement organisation.

Gandhi and Martin Luther King Jr. became such towering figures within their own movements that some people have the impression that successful nonviolence depends on 'charismatic' leadership. For us in WRI, however, nonviolent action is a source of social empowerment that strengthens the capacities of all participants without depending on superhuman leaders. Therefore we have advocated more participatory forms of decision-making, promoted adopting forms of organisation based on affinity groups (see p71), and expanded nonviolence training (see p27) to include tools for participatory strategy assessment and development.

Organising

Sometimes, it seems that nonviolence just happens, that thousands of people converge to do something. But usually this takes organisation, especially if the action is not simply reacting to some event publicised in all the mass media but a step in a campaign, an effort to set an agenda for social change. The image from outside might be of a more of less unified set of people. However, closer in, you see that the movement consists of various networks that each reach out through particular constituencies, of distinct organisations with their own themes and emphases, of several inter-connected campaigns taking up aspects of an issue. Nonviolent attitudes, methods of organisation, and forms of action strengthen the ability of these diverse elements to act in concert and to win new supporters.

Case Study: Nonviolence Training During the U.S. Civil Rights Movements

In 1942, radical pacifists formed the Nonviolent Action Committee of the Fellowship of Reconciliation, which trained teams to provide leadership in antiracist and antimilitarist work. Out of that grew the Congress of Racial Equality (CORE), which in 1945 became the first organisation to develop nonviolence trainings in preparation for involvement in the civil rights movement. For 10 years, beginning in 1947, CORE ran month-long training workshops in Washington, DC. Participants learned theories and skills in nonviolence and organising, with the goal of ending segregation in the capital area.

Early in the civil rights movement, the Southern Christian Leadership Conference based its preparation for nonviolent action campaigns (such as the 1956 Montgomery Bus Boycott) on African-American religious traditions. At mass meetings held in local churches, Martin Luther King Jr. and others lectured on nonviolence. Singing and prayer strengthened community spirit and the nonviolent discipline. As civil disobedience became a crucial part of the civil rights movement, training included role plays and signing a pledge to remain nonviolent.

It took extensive trainings to prepare civil rights workers for the violence they would encounter in the South. Participants in the Mississippi Freedom Summer of 1964 began with a two-week training. The Poor People's Campaign of 1968 held training programs for marchers, marshals, and support people.

✱ *Excerpted from* Decedes of Nonviolence Training: Practicing Nonviolence *by Joanne Sheehan from the* Nonviolent Activist, *July-August 1998.* *http://www.warresisters.org/nva0798-4.htm*

WHITE SOUTHERNERS POUR SUGAR, KETCHUP, AND MUSTARD OVER THE HEADS OF CIVIL RIGHTS DEMONSTRATORS DURING A LUNCH COUNTER SIT-IN IN JACKSON, MISSISSIPPI, USA, JUNE 12, 1963.
PHOTO: WIDE WORLD

Case Study: Otpor: People's Power in Serbia

OTPOR DRUMMERS LIVEN UP A DEMO IN BELGARDE, SERBIA   PHOTO: OTPOR

Within two years of its founding in 1998, the Serbian youth group Otpor (Resist) played a central role in bringing down Slobodan Miloševic. Initially their campaign aimed to change attitudes towards resisting Miloševic, for instance by using nonviolent 'guerilla' tactics of communication (graffiti, street theatre, etc.), often using humour to attract interest and to reduce fear. Increasingly, they put pressure on the divided democratic opposition and found points of unity to counter Miloševic and to undermine 'the pillars of his power'.

Nonviolence training workshops played an important role in spreading an understanding of how they could weaken the regime. When Miloševic did try to steal the elections, they were in a position to expose him and ultimately to stop him. When crowds surrounded the parliament building, the police were unwilling to disperse them. The most famous image is of a bulldozer driving into the parliament; by that time, the police made no effort to prevent this. The next day Miloševic resigned.

Otpor had played a vital role in achieving a necessary step in democratising Serbia — removing Miloševic — but subsequent progress towards democracy has been disappointing.

Resources

■ *Bringing Down a Dictator*, DVD, 60 minutes, a production of York Zimmerman Inc., Washington, D.C., USA
■ Albert Cevallos, *Whither the Bulldozer?: Nonviolent Revolution and the Transition to Democracy in Serbia* (US Institute of Peace special report No 72 — downloadable from http://www.usip.org)
■ The Website for the Centre for Applied NonViolent Action. Strategies includes articles by Otpor activists and others on their strategy and tactics: http://www.canvasopedia.org/content/serbian_case/otpor_strategy.htm

3

GENDER AND NONVIOLENCE

"Wars will cease when men refuse to fight — and women refuse to approve."

~ **Jesse Wallace Hughan, founder of War Resisters League**

I t may seem simple and obvious that we want both men and women involved in our struggles against war and injustice. However, if we want to fully utilise people's talents, energy, and insights, we need to apply gender awareness to how we organise ourselves, how we design our campaigns, and how we conduct our trainings for action.

Why? Because gender, our societies' definitions of male and female roles, of masculinity and femininity, influences all of us. And the social traditions that have constructed masculinity as dominant, aggressive, and controlling and femininity as weak, submissive, and serving have deeply affected each of us. Gender awareness helps us to make sure that in our nonviolent actions and campaigns, we don't perpetuate the same injustices we are trying to stop.

In antimilitarist campaigns, gender awareness and gender-based analysis are also valuable tools for creating an effective strategy. Gender is an element in every conflict. It may not be the cause of a conflict, but different ideas of masculinity and femininity are at the heart of why and how people fight. Military systems are built to function on certain ideas and assumptions about male and female roles. If we want to create nonviolent structures and systems for resolving conflict, we will need to create new assumptions and expectations about gender.

In this section, we include concepts and exercises to help you to incorporate gender awareness in your trainings and to examine your campaigns and nonviolent actions through a gender lens.

ASKING THE RIGHT QUESTIONS: NONVIOLENCE TRAINING AND GENDER, CHIANG MAI, THAILAND.
PHOTO: JOANNE SHEEHAN

What is Gender?

Gender is a social construction of ideas that defines the roles, belief systems and attitudes, images, values, and expectations of men and women. It contributes heavily to power relationships, not only between men and women, but also within each group; this results in many social problems. Different cultures have different ideas about gender, about what is suitable for men and women to do and to be. Gender not only changes from culture to culture, it also may change over time, or it may change within a culture during a crisis situation.

What is the Difference Between Gender and Sex?

Sex refers to natural biological differences between men and women. While many of these differences are clear and fixed, even some biological differences exist across a spectrum. Gender, however, is very much constructed by the cultural ideals, belief systems, images, and expectations about masculinity and femininity in a given society.

How is Gender Related to Power and Justice?

In many cultures, men's experiences and perspectives are seen as the norm. Heterosexual masculine behaviour, however that may be defined, is taken as the standard. The exercise of power, especially in public, is seen as masculine. In most cultures, men are assumed to be the leaders of family, community, and society while women are assumed to be followers and supporters. Such assumptions can mean that women and girls have little say in decisions that affect their lives. It can also mean that men who do not follow traditional roles face public criticism. However, because gender is a socially constructed idea, it is possible to challenge and change oppressive notions about male and female roles. This is what we call gender justice.

How Does Gender Affect Each of Us?

We are affected by social constructs about gender from the moment we are born. Masculinity is injected into boys' mentality in many ways. There are social pressures on them to deny their feelings, to act strong physically, and to prove their worth by dominating or competing with others. Control or power over others and violence may be seen as signs of masculinity. Such socialisation undermines the human dignity of everyone. Men and boys are often brutalised to prepare them for military service. War itself is gender violence against men, as men and boys are forced to kill.

Girls are often socialised to deny their intellects, to be good listeners, to be proper and obedient, and to prove their worth by placing the needs of others first. Passivity and silently accepting injustice may be seen as signs of femininity. Such socialisation undermines human dignity and fosters victimisation. Protection of women and girls is used in propaganda to incite or justify war. War itself is gender violence against women, as sexual violence is used as a weapon of war.

Why Should Peace Movements Deal with Gender Violence?

A gender perspective gives important insights into the work for peace and justice. Ideas about masculinity and femininity lie at the roots of violence and are used to support armed conflicts. The level of violence against women and girls in peacetime is an important indicator about how just and peaceful a society really is. Peace and justice organisations that want to end the violence of war will be more effective if they understand the full spectrum of violence in their society and challenge it.

Survivors of gender violence during war know that reconciliation is impossible without gender justice. The silence around sexual violence against men and boys during war must also be broken. Peace movements cannot ignore issues related to gender and war, such as the increased militarisation of women, the skills and leadership that women and girls could bring to peace-building, and how gender expectations encourage men to fight.

Why is a Gender Perspective Important in Our Work?

People who work for social change often assume that we are free from internalised assumptions about gender and thus do not need to learn and change ourselves. Creating awareness and changing ourselves and the dynamics within our organisations on gender issues is an important personal and organisational transformation that in itself acts to dismantle structural violence in the society.

It is difficult to work on gender issues because it is about everyone of us, and we cannot avoid it. Because we are directly affected, we often face fear when the issue is raised. We don't know how to deal with it or don't want to, and we are afraid of more conflict and division. Often it is easier to say that this is not our priority. To encourage ourselves, we can look for examples where other groups and movements have begun to raise these questions.

An Example of Linking Peace and Gender Issues: New Profile in Israel

How does a peace group interweave gender awareness into its peace work? This can be done through its organisational identity and structures, its training and orientation of members, and its development of program strategies.

New Profile, the Israeli peace organisation, describes itself as 'a group of feminist women and men who are convinced that we need not live in a soldiers' state'. Such a clear identification publicises the connections between gender and peace from the very beginning, for anyone who comes in contact with the organisation. New Profile breaks traditional organisational patterns by rotating leadership roles and all paid functions and tries to avoid having a hierarchy of activities. The group's many training and educational programs for new members and the public — workshops, seminars, youth groups, and conferences — always include an analysis of how gender and militarism are connected in Israeli culture and society. It also conductS whole-day study circles that look more deeply at the connections. One such study day in 2007, for example, used photographs of female soldiers from the army's archives to look at the the military recruitment of women in Israel and the general militarisation of the whole society. With such opportunities for study and discussion, New Profile members bring a deeper gender awareness to their problem analysis of militarism and their strategic action planning. New Profile's Small Arms and Light Weapons project not only looked into the problems and structure of the Israeli arms trade, but also investigated how small arms affected individual's lives and how New Profile could help redefine the term 'security' in Israeli culture.

Notes

■ Adapted from materials created by the International Fellowship of Reconciliation's Women Peacemakers Program (http://www.ifor.org/WPP/index.html) and expanded in the training manual of the International Women's Partnership for Peace and Justice (http://www.womenforpeaceandjustice.org/)

■ For more on New Profile, see article on p101.

4

TASKS AND TOOLS
FOR ORGANISING AND
FACILITATING TRAININGS

Planning and facilitating nonviolence training requires a range of tasks that a number of people should share. First, campaign organisers need to be aware of when and what training is needed. Does the group need training in strategic campaign development or gender sensitivity? Is training needed to prepare a new group of people to participate in nonviolent actions or for an experienced group to achieve new skills? Do affinity groups need training in group process?

Once a decision is made to have a training, trainers are needed. As stated in 'Nonviolence Training' (p13), if trainers are not available, create a team of co-facilitators to do the training. This section has check-lists to help organise, plan, and facilitate trainings.

Organisers and trainers need to talk together before working on their own tasks. A lack of clarity and assumptions made by trainers or organisers can result in an ineffective training. A training can be an important opportunity to test plans, to find weaknesses in the group, or to bring more people into the process. A trainer must be open to those goals.

If the trainers are part of the group, they need to be clear about their role as trainers. While they understand the context, the group, the campaign, the action scenario, etc. better than an outside facilitator, trainers deeply involved in the work can have difficulty stepping into a different role; clarifying roles should help in that process.

✷ The 'Nonviolent Campaigns' (p31) and 'Organising for Effective Nonviolent Actions' (p57) sections include information that can help trainers and organisers understand what they need to do and what they may need to train for.

WOMEN ACTIVISTS AND TRAINERS PARTICPATE IN GENDER-SPECIFIC NONVIOLENCE AND EMPOWERMENT TRAINING, HELD OUTSIDE THE UK'S NUCLEAR WEAPONS FACTORY - AWE ALDERMASTON, UK.
PHOTO: JUDITH BARON

Working Together

1) Several of the organisers and all the trainers should meet well in advance to plan the training. Depending on the situation, the organisers may need to go back to the group for further decision-making. The trainers' questions may help the organisers understand what more they need to do to prepare the group for the training.
2) Discuss how much time is needed to accomplish the goals of the training. Can it be done in one day (how many hours) or a weekend? Can the training be done in steps, following the process of campaign development? Do you need a series of trainings to plan a campaign? Some groups take a holiday week to plan and prepare for a campaign. If people are travelling to an action, how can you plan for training?
3) Trainers need information about the participants: are they people coming together just for this action or do they meet regularly? What level of experience do they have? Have they done trainings before? Have they done nonviolent actions and what kinds?
4) Discuss the group's approach to nonviolence and training. Does it have nonviolence guidelines? (See p32.)
5) Ask the campaign organisers to present specific information at the training (e.g., scenario plans, campaign background). Be clear how much time they have for this task.
6) Identify what handouts are needed; use maps and pictures if appropriate.
7) Be clear who is responsible for bringing supplies (markers, paper, tape, photocopies of handouts, copies of the handbook, equipment for films, etc.) and arrangements for food or other physical needs.

Check-List for Organising a Training

1) Make sure that the space where the training will occur has enough room for people to do role plays and exercises, to sit in a circle, and that it is accessible to those coming.
2) Make sure there is a wall board or paper to write on.
3) Food and beverages are important; make sure someone is responsible for it or that participants are asked to bring something to share.
4) Outreach should include a clear description of the training and the need for full participation, its length, etc.

Check-List for Facilitating a Training

1) Facilitators should realise that it may take as long to prepare for as to actually present/facilitate the training. It is important that co-facilitators work together to build the agenda and are clear who is responsible for what and how they will work together.
2) Be realistic about the amount of time allotted for each section. Don't give in to the pressure to do the training quickly if it can't be done.
3) Start the training with introductions. Break the ice with introductory exercises. If the group members know each other well, ask a question so people learn something new about each other.
4) If trainers don't have enough information about people's experiences, use non-competitive ways to ask. Set a tone, explaining that the trainers need the information but that it is not an exercise in identifying who is 'better'.
5) Early in the training, have exercises that will encourage participation, such as a simple hassle line (see p120).
6) Balance activity in pairs or trios with activity in larger groups.
7) Mix discussion with moving exercises; provide regular breaks.
8) Keep track of time, and mark possible cuts if you get behind schedule. But don't cut the last items as they may be some of the most important, such as the scenario role play.
9) Always leave time for evaluation, and use different forms of evaluation. Write on wall charts 'what went well' (+) and 'what could have been better' (>). Ask a series of questions to solicit comments; use a go around or a brainstorm method. Written evaluation forms are very helpful for long trainings.

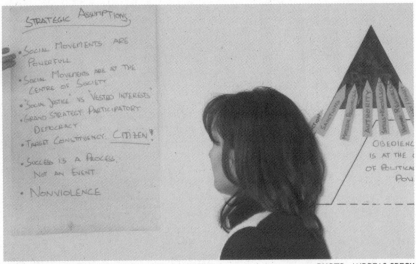

CAMPAIGN DEVELOPMENT TRAINING, TIBLISI, GEORGIA. PHOTO: ANDREAS SPECK

5

NONVIOLENT CAMPAIGNS

What Makes a Campaign Nonviolent

Whether or not it includes a clear commitment to nonviolence, most of the basic steps in campaigns are the same: research and collect information, educate and train, develop a strategy. What, then, is unique about a 'nonviolent campaign'? It's certainly more than simply not being violent.

Many organisations and campaigns committed to nonviolence have statements of their nonviolent principles that explain their perspectives. WRI's Statement of Principles describes what we mean when we say we embrace nonviolence:

'Nonviolence can combine active resistance, including civil disobedience, with dialogue; it can combine non-cooperation-withdrawal of support from a system of oppression-with constructive work to build alternatives. As a way of engaging in conflict, sometimes nonviolence attempts to bring reconciliation with it: strengthening the social fabric, empowering those at the bottom of society, and including people from different sides in seeking a solution. Even when such aims cannot immediately be achieved, our nonviolence holds us firm in our determination not to destroy other people'. (http://wri-irg.org/statemnt/stprinc-en.htm)

The following list identifies specific principles particular to nonviolence. While some of these may be found in campaigns that do not identify as being nonviolent, the combination of these principles makes a campaign nonviolent.

Principles of Nonviolent Action

These Principles were developed through a collaborative process, involving nonviolence trainers in the United States and the editorial committee of this Handbook. We encourage you to use this, or another set of principles, to stimulate discussion within your group. Use the 'Spectrum/Barometer' Exercise (p140) to help your group understand where members stand in relation to nonviolence principles. If there are large differences, you will need to discuss how that will affect your nonviolent campaign. The use of Nonviolent Guidelines may be the best way to define your agreements as a group (at least for the purposes of your campaign).

- We acknowledge the value of each person. This is fundamental: recognising the dignity and humanity of oneself and others. We refuse to mistreat our opponent as an enemy.
- We recognise that we all have part of the truth; no one has all of it. No one is all 'right' or all 'wrong'. Our campaign information gathering, educations, and actions should reflect this.
- Our actions emphasise openness to promote communication and democratic processes. We work for processes that express 'power with' not 'power over' others. Empowering all involved in a campaign is important. We promote democratic structures (internally and externally) to maximise self-determination.
- Our means (behaviours and actions) are consistent with our ends (of affirming life, opposing oppression and seeking justice, valuing every person). Our strategy must be based on this principle, we cannot justify a 'victory' obtained through violent or deceitful methods.
- We are willing to undergo suffering rather than inflict it. Refusing to inflict suffering is based on the value of each person and is a strategy that draws attention to our commitment and our cause. We will not violently fight back if attacked. We recognise jail may be a consequence of our actions; filling the jails may be a strategy.
- We commit to prepare ourselves for nonviolent action according to the guidelines agreed. If necessary, we will attempt to arrange orientation sessions or workshops in nonviolence to better understand and practice this commitment.

> ✳ *Find Martin Luther King, Jr's principles of nonviolence at:*
> *http://www.thekingcenter.org/prog/non/6principles.html*

Nonviolence Guidelines

Going back to the Code of Discipline laid down by Gandhi in the 1930's, many campaigns have developed 'nonviolence guidelines' to which all participants are asked to agree. 'Nonviolence guidelines' are not the same as nonviolent principles. They are agreements on how participants in an action will behave. They may be stated in very practical terms ('We will not carry any weapons') or may be in more philosophical terms ('We will gather together in a manner that reflects the world we choose to create').

Agreeing on what we mean by 'nonviolence' or why we choose nonviolence should not be assumed. Even in a small and apparently homogeneous group, discussion will bring up different interpretations and varied levels of commitment to nonviolence. Nonviolence guidelines make clear what is expected and set a nonviolent spirit for the action. In the midst of an action, it is easy for a

SCHOOL OF THE AMERICAS WATCH DEMONSTRATION, FORT BENNING, USA. PHOTO: JOANNE SHEEHAN

crowd's tone to move in the direction of verbal abuse and even violence. Government infiltrators may attempt to discredit a group by urging people to act violently. Nonviolent agreements, and nonviolence training, can make it possible for a large number of people to participate in a campaign nonviolently, even if they have little experience in this area. No matter how committed the organisers are to the principles of nonviolent action and how well the campaign strategy is organised, it is crucial that the participants in demonstrations and civil disobedience actions to reflect the principles of nonviolence for it to be an effective nonviolent campaign.

Examples of nonviolence guidelines

- Faslane 365:
  http://www.faslane365.org/fr/display_preview/nonviolence_guidelines
- Lakenheath Action Group:
  http://www.motherearth.org/lakenheathaction/nv.php3
- School of the Americas Watch:
  http://www.soaw.org/article.php?id=1093
- Principles of the Students' Union of the University of Prishtina, 1997:
  http://wri-irg.org/wiki/index.php/Principles_of_the_Students%27_Union
  _of_the_University_of_Prishtina%2C_1997

Planning Nonviolent Campaigns

Demonstrations alone do not end a particular war or correct a deep-rooted injustice. Faced with the horrors of the world, it's easy to do the nonviolent equivalent of lashing out – jumping into action or activity without stepping back or looking ahead. Too often groups go directly from recognising a problem to picking a tactic. Or we suffer from the 'paralysis of analysis', educating ourselves and others, but never getting to action, and therefore never reaching our goals. The power of a nonviolent campaign comes in creatively combining tactics, strategic thinking, and participants' commitment.

Influencing change on a specific issue usually requires a campaign, that is a connected series of activities and actions carried out over a period of time to achieve specific, stated goals. Campaigns are started by a group of people with a common concern. The participants develop a common understanding and vision, identify goals, and begin the process of research, education, and training that strengthens and expands the number of participants who engage in the activities and action.

A campaign has goals on different levels. First is a specific campaign demand or stated goal. Most campaigns challenge the policies of people at the top of some hierarchy. To reach this goal, we need to bring a new factor into their decision-making—be that persuading them with new information, convincing those on whose support they depend, or warning them of the resistance they will face. We do not treat them as enemies, but as adversaries—people who have to be stopped or moved in order for us to end a specific injustice.

A campaign also has internal goals such as building the capacity of and number of participants. A nonviolent campaign takes people through processes of empowerment. This involves personal empowerment (people discovering and exercising their own power against oppression, exclusion, and violence, and for participation, peace, and human rights) and builds collective power. Groups learn how to be organisers and become political strategists in the process.

Campaigns should also communicate something of the vision of what we want, leading to further campaigns that challenge existing power structures. Multiple campaigns can move us towards the social empowerment that leads to the social transformation we are working for. In our training and planning we need to consider all aspects of this nonviolent social empowerment process: personal empowerment, community power, people power.

To develop an effective nonviolent strategy we need to develop strategic thinking skills.

Developing effective strategies

Creative campaigns hold the key to exploring the potential of nonviolence. And when groups are excited about the power and possibilities of a nonviolent campaign, they are more likely to develop an effective campaign strategy. The exercises suggested below can help produce that enthusiasm and excitement; they also offer suggestions on making campaigns effective as well as an understanding of how change happens.

If you are working for social change in your community, you may want to undertake a group process to prepare an effective strategy for moving towards this change. A group process draws on the resources already in the group and can generate enthusiasm and commitment.

To begin, you may want to have the group share its own knowledge of campaigns, using either the '10/10 Strategies' (p125) exercise or discussing how change happens by asking participants what effective campaigns they know about and what made them effective. Create a check-list from the responses. Case studies (see 'Campaign Case Study Guide', p54) are another way of learning from what has been done in the past. They do not offer blueprints, but show the determination, resourcefulness, and patience of successful nonviolent campaigns. See the Resources section (Section Eleven) for films and books that describe nonviolent campaigns or use some of the stories told in this Handbook or in the Weblinks.

If your group has a great amount of knowledge, you have limited time, or another factor makes this type of historical review not feasible, you can move right into developing your own process for a successful strategy for change. In order to develop effective strategies, a useful process is to:

■ name and describe the problem or situation
■ analyse why it exists
■ create a vision of what the group wants, including clear goals and
■ develop a strategy to reach those goals.

These steps are explained below.

Name and Describe the problem

For many who face problems in their daily lives, describing and analysing problems is a natural part of the process of living. But others need to be more intentional about it. These steps are intended to help people move together in a non-hierarchical, inclusive process to a deeper understanding of effective nonviolent strategies.

Naming and describing the problem or situation may seem too simple a first step for some, but if it is not done collectively, people may have different assumptions, different descriptions, and therefore different messages and goals. And we can't analyse without clarity about what we are analysing. Going through this process together strengthens the participation of the individuals while developing collective action.

 Exercises: A group can choose either 'The Tree' (p126) or 'The Pillars of Power' (p128) exercise to use throughout the strategic thinking and planning process, depending on which seems more suitable to their issue and their style.

Analyse why the problem exists

To transform a problem situation, we need to understand why it exists and who potentially supports and opposes it. We need to analyse the power structure to find entry points for resistance, constructive work, etc. An analysis should consider the following questions:

■ Do we understand the context and the root causes of the problem?
■ Who benefits and who suffers from it and how?
■ Who holds the power, and who has the power to create change? (Who forms part of the structures underpinning this? Who opposes this?)
■ Is there a difference between male and female roles? (See also Section Three, 'Gender and Nonviolence'.)
■ What are the strengths, weaknesses, opportunities, and threats for a campaign to change this? (SWOT analysis)
■ What theories do we bring to this analysis?
■ How does our commitment to nonviolent social change affect our analysis?

 Exercises: Continue to use either 'The Tree' (p126) or 'The Pillars' (p128). To look more deeply at those who support and oppose the structure, use the 'Spectrum of Allies' (p130) exercise, which helps us identify and analyse the players and our allies and opponents and helps in making strategic decisions regarding who we want to move.

Create a Vision of What We Want

To move forward, a campaign needs a vision of what it wants. Otherwise actions can simply be reactions, protests easy to disregard. A vision is likely to include ambitious long-term goals. It is worth asking groups to discuss their vision of big questions: world peace, economic justice, the society we want. The challenge then, however, is to identify the first steps in those journeys: the short − and medium-range goals that lead towards these long-term goals. Campaigns face dilemmas in setting goals. To get the maximum possible support, a campaign might choose a short-term goal as a 'lowest common denominator' − that is, a point upon which a wide range of people can agree. However, if this does not have deeper implications, if it does not suggest further steps for social transformation, then any change that results is likely to be shallow and unsatisfactory. On the other hand, utopian goals that seem unrealistic are not likely to mobilise people unless there are more attainable intermediate objectives. When the ultimate goals are revolutionary, campaigns need to identify limited, but more acceptable, stepping stones.

Questions to consider while developing goals:

■ Are the goals realistic; can they be achieved in a certain period of time?
■ Will people believe they can achieve this goal?
■ Does the goal match the group's purpose and capacity?
■ Are the goals measurable; will we know when we have achieved them?
■ Are the goals relevant to people's lives; will they be moved to participate?
■ Will people feel empowered by the 'victory'?

Exercises: Envision a Healthy Tree — Use the questions in 'The Tree' exercise (p126). Can we answer the above questions positively? 'The Pillars of Power' (p128) — What are the short — and medium-range goals that weaken the pillars? What do we aim to do with the underlying principles? Can we answer the above questions positively? (For more information on messages, also see 'Messaging' in 'The Role of Media', p49, and 'Sending the Protest Message', p57.)

Develop a Strategy

Once you have described and analysed the problem, a vision of what you want, and goals to move you towards that, you need to develop a strategy — a plan — to get there. Strategy development is not done in one meeting or by one person. It is a process of decision-making, organising, mobilising, and developing creative strategies.

What follows are the basic components of a nonviolent campaign. The 'Stories and Strategies' (Section Eight) describe how many of these components were used in campaigns.

Components of a Campaign

The following questions can help you and your group in the process of developing a campaign strategy. You and your group need to do this work on an ongoing basis, not just at the beginning of a campaign. This Handbook includes many resources to help you through the process.

Common Understanding

Is there a common understanding of the problem or situation that exists? Have we analysed why it exists? Does the analysis include the social, economic, and political structures? Do we have a common understanding of what it means to have a nonviolent campaign? Do we have an agreed upon decision-making process?

Nonviolent Discipline

Have the organisers discussed and agreed to nonviolent principles? Are there nonviolence guidelines? Are these clearly stated for all to understand? (See 'Principles of Nonviolent Action,' p31, and 'Nonviolence Guidelines', p32)

Research and Information Gathering

What do we know, and what do we need to know? Are we searching for the truth or just trying to 'prove our side'? Who can gather the information we need? Who can guide us and provide sources? Research includes finding out how others think about the issue. Listening Projects Community Surveys (see http://www.listeningproject.info) are one way to do that. Listening

Projects help activists look more deeply at an issue, gathering information on which to base future strategy while developing a connection between those being interviewed and those listening. Listening projects have been done in Cambodia, Croatia, Cambodia, South Africa, and the United States.

Education

Is the information understandable for the people we are trying to reach? A role of nonviolent activists is to put the research in a form that can be widely used in a campaign, or facilitate people through that process. Are we using popular education and conscientisation processes? Have we developed good educational materials, considering the different constituencies and allies we want to reach? What other educational processes can we use (e.g., street theatre)? How are we using the media to raise awareness?

Training

Do we need training to learn the skills to develop strategy and organise (e.g., group process, strategic planning, media work)? Are we providing training to prepare people for nonviolent action? Is training available to everyone? Do our trainings address issues of oppression and how we deal with them both in a societal context and within our groups and relationships? (See Section Four, as well as the 'Speak Out', p122, and 'A Gender Dialogue for Peacebuilders', p124, Exercises.)

Allies

Who are our allies; who might become allies or supporters if we communicate with them more? How do we reach out and build cooperative relationships with groups with whom we want to work in coalition? (Use the 'Spectrum of Allies', p130, Exercise to identify potential allies.)

Negotiation

Have we clearly identified who we need to negotiate with? How will we communicate with them? Are we clear what we want? Are we clear that our aims are not to humiliate our opponent but to work for a peaceful solution?

Constructive Work/Alternative Institutions

Gandhi saw constructive programmes (see 'Constructive Programme', p40) as the beginning of building a new society, even in the shell of the old. A key element of social change, it is designed to meet the needs of a population (e.g., economic equality, communal unity, developing local industries) and to develop community. Constructive work is often missing in campaigns in the West and emphasised in the East. While we say 'no' to an injustice, how do we say 'yes'? How do we begin building the vision of what we are working towards?

Alternative institutions may be temporary creations, such as setting up alternative transportation while boycotting a segregated/apartheid bus system.

Legislative and Electoral Action

Is legislative or electoral action part of the campaign, either as an educational tactic or a goal? How will we put pressure on politicians? How do we exercise our power? How will people participate in that action? What are our plans if our goals are not met?

Demonstrations

How can we best demonstrate our concerns? Have we considered the many methods of nonviolent action? (See 'Forms of Action', p46.) Are we clear about the objectives of the demonstration and how they will help us reach our goals? How will we involve the public? Will our actions make sense to the local community?

Nonviolent Direct Action/Civil Disobedience/Civil Resistance

Have we done all we can to build support for our action? Will it encourage more community involvement or will it be counter-productive? How will it advance our cause rather than be an end in itself? Are our objectives clear? Will it put the kind of pressure on our adversaries that will influence them to move? Who will it pressure?

In his *Letter from a Birmingham Jail*, Martin Luther King Jr. wrote, 'You may well ask, "Why direct action? Why sit-ins, marches, etc.? Isn't negotiation a better path?" You are exactly right in your call for negotiation. Indeed, this is the purpose of direct action. Nonviolent direct action seeks to create such a crisis and establish such creative tension that a community that has constantly refused to negotiate is forced to confront the issue. It seeks so to dramatise the issue that it can no longer be ignored.'

 Exercise: write this quote on a wall chart. Ask the group to identify the crisis, the creative tension, the community, and how they can dramatise the issue in their campaign. See also 'Stages of Escalation', p47.

Reconciliation

'As a way of engaging in conflict, sometimes nonviolence attempts to bring reconciliation with it: strengthening the social fabric, empowering those at the bottom of society, and including people from different sides in seeking a solution'. (WRI Statement of Principles) Have we been working for a win-win, rather than a win-lose situation? Is the reconciliation public or private? (In some successful nonviolent campaigns in the U.S. Civil Rights Movement white businessmen asked that restaurant integration be done without a public statement to avoid a negative reaction, while in other cases a public event demonstrated the desegregation of a system.)

Celebrate

When we reach our goals, let's take time to recognise what we have done and celebrate our achievements. Sometimes we reach beyond our goals, or accomplish other goals, and don't take the time to understand that. Collective evaluation is vital; by documenting our successes and failures and sharing with others we have sources to learn from when we take steps towards our next goal. If key activists are tired or burnt out, they may not see what is being achieved. Some compulsive types may also not accept that a campaign is stuck and may need some help to see that the best part of banging your head against a brick wall is when you stop.

Evaluate

We have a lot to consider when developing strategic nonviolent campaigns. We need to learn to think strategically, to develop our understanding of the power of nonviolence, and to go through the steps that can move us effectively to our goals. This should strengthen and empower our community along the way. It's important to evaluate our campaign, not just at the end, but as we go through it. Unless we do so, we may be making mistakes that we will not recognise until it is too late. We should listen to everyone involved. Keeping a record of our meetings, our decisions, and our work becomes the basis of our own case study. Whether we were successful or not, we can learn from our experiences. And it's crucial so we can share our strategies and stories.

* See 'Action Evaluation', p90 and 'Campaign Case Study Guide', p54.

Constructive Programme

According to Gandhi, nonviolent social change requires building a new society in the shell of the old, which he termed constructive programme. 'Nonviolence for Gandhi was more than just a technique of struggle or a strategy for resisting military aggression,' Robert Burrowes explains in his 1995 study, The Strategy of Nonviolent Defense: A Gandhian Approach. Rather, 'it was intimately related to the wider struggle for social justice, economic self-reliance, and ecological harmony as well as the quest for self-realization.' As Burrowes describes it: 'For the individual, [constructive programme] meant increased power-from-within through the development of personal identity, self-reliance, and fearlessness. For the community, it meant the creation of a new set of political, social, and economic relations'. In cases where political revolutions have taken place but the population was not organised to exercise self-determination, creating a new society has been extremely difficult, and a new dictatorship usurping power has too often resulted.

Gandhi posited three elements needed for social transformation: personal transformation, political action, and constructive programme. He saw them as

YOUTH BUILDING BOXES FROM SINCELEJO, COLOMBIA.   PHOTO: PAZ CARIBE SINCELEJO

intertwined, all equally necessary to achieve social change. The core elements that Gandhi saw as necessary for transforming and liberating India involved pro-grammes to embody equality, liberate education, promote economic self-reliance, and create a clean environment. Equality meant creating ashrams, political campaigns, and cooperative enterprises across social divides. They would cut through communal lines (Hindu/Muslim/Sikh, etc.), gender inequal-ity, and caste distinctions — especially 'untouchability' — and include members of the 'hill tribes' and people suffering from leprosy. Gandhi began education projects: literacy campaigns to promote basic reading and math skills, political education, knowledge about health, and nonviolence training for students. His economic self-reliance campaigns involved, most famously, spinning homemade cloth, which was done throughout India. A constructive programme that was often done collectively, it was also a campaign of non-cooperation with Indians' systematic dependency on the British for cloth. Economic self-reliance also involved diversifying crops, creating village industries, and developing labour unions. Environmental efforts involved the whole community in village sanita-tion, which meant, for Hindus, overtly flouting caste norms.

The process of working on constructive programme has fundamental bene-fits, the first of which is providing immediate assistance to those in greatest need. As people come together in community, not individual, action, they build constituencies for social change. Gandhi saw constructive programme as train-ing for civil disobedience, which often included non-cooperation. Constructive work provides opportunities to develop the skills needed to build a new society.

Examples of Constructive Programmes

Colombia

Since the year 2000, Sincelejo, a small Caribbean town in Colombia, has been the second largest city receiving displaced people from the Colombian conflict. The youth in this town have faced forced recruitment by the state army, the rebel groups, and the paramilitary. Many of them have joined these forces because of economic reasons, to support their families. The conscientious objection group from Sincelejo started creating alternatives against forced recruitment, first by giving workshops on peace culture, nonviolence, and conscientious objection. Then, as they realised that economics were a main reason why the youth in Sincelejo were recruited, they started creating economic alternatives by forming their own small enterprises. The group now produces cartons and boxes, organic vegetables, margarine, t-shirts, and bakery goods which bring an income to them and their families. The main aims of these effort are:

- to prevent the recruitment of youth
- to form a support network to prevent forced recruitment
- to form youngsters in nonviolent methods for resolving conflicts
- to come up with economic strategies to support the basic needs of their families.

Kenya

Far-sighted as is Wangari Maathai, the founder of the Green Belt movement in Kenya, not even she could see in 1976 where a simple constructive activity such as tree-planting would lead. She first proposed this to the Kenyan National Council of Women as an activity to carry out in cooperation with the government forestry commission that provided the seeds. Through this, she argued, women could address some of the economic problems urgently affecting their lives. She had no idea that the expansion of this network would lead in the 1990s to the Green Belt Movement being in the forefront of national campaigns against corruption and for multi-party democracy, in which she herself was beaten and jailed, or that later that she would be a leading spokeswoman in the world campaign to write off 'third world' debt.

United States

The nonviolence movement in the West has not emphasised constructive programme, but has focused more on protest, yet examples of constructive programmes in the United States include community land trusts for permanently affordable housing, worker-owned cooperatives, battered women's shelters and rape crisis centres, an amplified interest in alternative public schools, urban gardens, local food production without pesticides, the viral spread of free and open-source software and art, and affordable renewable energy. Constructive programme is more than constructing new things. Many aspects of Gandhi's programme focused on moving toward equality. In the United States that means serious anti-oppression work, as well as dealing with economic inequalities. While there is poverty in the United States and a growing gap between the rich and the poor, constructive programmes need to support reducing materialistic consumption.

Bill Moyer's Movement Action Plan (MAP)

'The Movement Action Plan provides activists with a practical, how-to-do-it analytic tool for evaluating and organising social movements that are focused on national and international issues, such as nuclear energy and weapons, non-intervention in Central America, civil and human rights, AIDS, democracy and freedom, apartheid, or ecological responsibility.

MAP describes eight stages through which social movements normally progress over a period of years and decades. For each state, MAP describes the role of the public, powerholders, and the movement. It provides organizers with a map of the long road of successful movements, which helps them guide their movement along the way.

Most social movements are not just in one stage. Movements usually have many demands for policy changes, and their efforts for each demand are in a specific stage.

For each of the movement's major demands or goals, MAP enables activists to evaluate the movement and identify which stage it is in; identify successes already achieved; develop effective strategies, tactics, and programmes; establish short and long-term goals; and avoid common pitfalls.

Social movements do not fit neatly into MAP's eight stages or move through them in a linear way. Social movements are more dynamic. Movements have a number of different demands, and the effort for each demand is in a different MAP stage. When movements achieve one demand, they focus on achieving other demands that are at earlier stages.

Finally, MAP is only a theoretical model, built from past experience. Real-life social movements will neither fit exactly nor move through the stages linearly, smoothly, or precisely in the manner outlined.

The purpose of MAP is to give activists hope and empowerment, increase the effectiveness of social movements, and reduce the discouragement that often contributes to individual burnout, dropout, and the winding down of social movements.'

■ http://historyisaweapon.com/defcon1/moyermap.html
■ charts: http://www.nonviolence.org.au/downloads/moyer_charts.pdf

* See over for 'eight stages' diagram

1. Normal Times

- A critical social problem exists that violates widely held values;
- Powerholders support problem: Their "Official Policies" tout widely held values, but the "Operating Policies" violate those values;
- Public is unaware of the problem and supports powerholders
- Problem/policies not a public issue;

2. Prove the Failure of official Institutions

- Many new local opposition groups;
- Use official channels - courts, government offices, commissions, hearings, etc. - to prove they don't work;
- Become experts; do research;

Eight Stages of the Process of Social Movement Success

Campaigns

CHARACTERISTICS OF MOVEMENT PROCESS

- Social movements are composed of many sub-goals and sub-movements, each in their own MAP stage;
- Strategy and tactics are different for each sub-movement, according to the MAP stage each is in;
- Keep advancing sub-movements through the Eight Stages;
- Each sub-movement is focused on a specific goal (e.g., for civil rights movements: restaurants, voting, public accommodation)
- All of the sub-movements promote the same paradigm shift (e.g., shift from hard to soft energy policy);

Public Must be Convinced Three Times
1. That there is a problem (Stage Four);
2. To oppose current conditions and policies (Stages Four, Six, Seven);
3. To want, no longer fear, alternatives (Stages Six, Seven)

8. Continuing the Struggle

- Extend successes (e.g., even stronger civil rights laws);
- Oppose attempts at backlash;
- Promote paradigm shift;
- Recognize/celebrate successes so far;

3. Ripening Conditions

- Recognition of problem and victims grows;
- Public sees victim's faces;
- More active local groups;
- Need pre-existing institutions and networks available to new movement;
- 20 to 30 percent of public opposes powerholder policies;

4. Take Off

- TRIGGER EVENT;
- **Dramatic nonviolent actions/campaigns;**
- **Actions show public that conditions and policies violate widely held values;**
- **Nonviolent actions repeated around country;**
- **Problem put on the social agenda;**
- **New social movement rapidly takes off;**
- **40 percent of public opposes current policies/conditions;**

PROTESTS

POWERHOLDERS

5. Perception of Failure

- See goals unachieved;
- See powerholders unchanged;
- See numbers down at demonstrations;
- Despair, hopelessness, burnout, dropout, seems movement ended;
- Emergence of negative rebel;

6. Majority Public Opinion

- Majority oppose present conditions and powerholder policies;
- Show how the problem and policies affect all sectors of society;
- Involve mainstream citizens and institutions in addressing the problem;
- Problem put on the political agenda;
- Promote alternatives;
- Counter each new powerholder strategy;
- Demonology: Powerholders promote public's fear of alternatives and activism;
- Promote a paradigm shift, not just reforms;
- Re-trigger events happen, re-enacting Stage Four for a short period;

7. Success

- Large majority oppose policies and no longer fear alternative;
- **Many powerholders split off and change positions;**
- **End-game process: Powerholders change policies (it's more costly to continue old policies than to change), are voted out of office, or slow, invisible attrition;**
- **New laws and policies;**
- **Powerholders try to make minimal reforms while movement demands social change;**

Forms of Nonviolent Action

Gene Sharp researched and catalogued 198 methods of nonviolent action which he first published in 1973 in *The Politics of Nonviolent Action*. These methods are broken into three broad classifications: Protest and Persuasion, Non-cooperation, and Nonviolent Intervention. These are further grouped into sections. The full list is available at http://www.aeinstein.org.

1. Protest and Persuasion

■ Demonstrations — Many people express what they want by walking together in the street, for example, the demonstrations against war on Iraq on the 15th of February 2003. The biggest anti-war demonstration ever, it occurred in more than 600 cities around the world. In London alone, two million people demonstrated.

■ Protest lists — Signing your name to a list to express dissent with a certain policy, for instance a protest against Swedish weapon exports to United States and Great Britain during the Iraq war.

2. Non-Cooperation

■ Boycott — To refuse to buy merchandise or a service to show dissatisfaction with the seller or government, for example, the boycott of South African products during the apartheid regime. Individuals and organisations first started to boycott South African merchandise; after a while, entire countries boycotted South Africa.

■ Strike — To refuse to work. For example during the first Intifada, the Palestinian resistance that started in 1987, most Palestinians refused to work for Israelis. Israel lost a lot of money without access to cheap Palestinian labour, and the economy stagnated.

■ Political non-cooperation — The refusal to do military service or to perform an extradition. War Resisters International is one of the organisations that supports those who want to refuse to do military service.

■ Refusal to cooperate — For example during the Second World War, Norwegian teachers refused to follow the Nazi curriculum for schools. They were sent to concentration camps because of their disobedience, but most of them were released when the Nazis understood that they wouldn't give in.

3. Intervention

■ Blockades — To place your body in the way of something. For example, Israelis and international volunteers block Israeli bulldozers that are about to demolish Palestinian homes.

■ Preventive Presence — To protect endangered persons in conflict areas, for example, peace observers in Mexico, Israel-Palestine, or Colombia.

■ Plowshares Actions — To openly disarm weapons and to be willing to take your sentence, for example, the disarming of Trident nuclear submarines in Scotland.

Stages of Escalation in a Nonviolent Campaign

When we develop and carry out a nonviolent campaign for social change, we need to go beyond publicising and protesting injustices, refusing to cooperate with oppressors, and intervening nonviolently. We need to implement constructive programmes as well, in which we actually live the change that is our goal.

The interrelationship between confrontational action and constructive action at different stages of a campaign is displayed in the chart 'Stages of Escalation of a Nonviolent Campaign' (see p47). This chart is based upon Theodor Ebert's book *Nonviolent Rebellion — Alternatives to Civil War*. The early stages of a nonviolent campaign emphasise bringing an issue into the public sphere. A well-organised campaign will use public protest actions and will also present possible alternatives (constructive action) to draw attention to the issues and to encourage change.

If this does not achieve the desired results, the campaign may move to 'stage 2'. In this stage, the campaign increases public pressure by staging legal forms of non-cooperation (strikes, consumer boycotts, slow-downs, etc.) as well as legal innovative activities (fair trade initiatives, alternative economy structures, nonviolent intervention, etc.). The goal at this stage is to raise the stakes (societal costs) and minimise the rewards for those committing or benefiting from the injustices. At the same time the campaign will most likely be continuing its actions from the first stage.

This might be sufficient to reach the desired goals. But if not, the participants have the possibility of using nonviolent actions that require much more risk from the activists and which also present a much more powerful statement to the public. The third stage of escalation would use nonviolent civil disobedience both as a protest (sit-ins, blockades, strikes, refusal to go to war) but also as civil usurpation, carrying out actions that exercise authority or implement a structure without a legal right to do so. Examples of this are providing sanctuary to prevent the deportation of refugees, nonviolent intervention, reverse strikes, or building an environmentally sound village on the construction site of an environmentally destructive factory.

As nonviolent campaigns develop, their strategies will escalate from one stage to the next, but they will continue to use actions from previous stages. This does not imply that there is a inflexible linear escalation. However, it is useful to show the interrelationship of these stages and types of actions. A campaign may consciously decide to move from one stage to another (up or down) as it chooses the most effective actions for the situation. Throughout a campaign it is important to make the effort to engage in dialogue with one's opponents, trying to find solutions that include all parties. At certain times, for example, this dialogue may start more easily if the campaign temporarily reduces its public pressure. A campaign may also decide that is more effective to increase its work on constructive action and to hold back on confrontational actions, or vice versa.

Carrying out a successful campaign requires an ongoing evaluation of the campaign's activities and their effectiveness. Your group can use the framework of this chart to track a campaign's implementation of constructive as well as confrontational actions over time to evaluate how they work together to achieve your goals.

Stages of Escalation of Nonviolent Campaigns

Stage of Escalation	Confrontational Action (actions that are directed against injustice in society)	Constructive Action (actions that help to construct a just order in society)	How it Works
Bring the issue into the public arena	**Protest** (demonstration, petition, leaflet, vigil)	**Presenting alternatives** (teach-in lectures, show alternatives)	Publicising / Convincing
Legal actions that deal with the issue	**Legal non-cooperation:** (strike, consumer boycott, go slow)	**Legal innovative activities** (fair trade, free schools, alternative economy, ethical investments, nonviolent intervention)	Raising the stakes (costs) and minimising the rewards for those committing injustice
Illegal actions that deal with the issue	**Civil disobedience:** (sit-in, blockade, tax resistance, strike, war resistance)	**Civil usurpation:** (sanctuary movement, pirate radio, reverse strike, nonviolent intervention)	Redirecting power

* *Adapted and translated from German into English by Eric Bachman. This is a direct translation of the* Chart of escalation of nonviolent actions *on page 37 of* Gewaltfreier Aufstand — Alternative zum Bürgerkrieg *(Nonviolent Rebellion — Alternatives to Civil War) by Theodor Elbert, Waldkircher Verlagsgesellschaft mbH, 1978, ISBN 3-870885-030-1.*

The Role of Media

Why should we use the media in our campaigns? Perhaps this is a strange way to begin this section of the Handbook, but it is an important question for groups to ask themselves before beginning a relationship with mainstream or alternative media outlets. The media is pervasive in modern life, especially in the western world, where images and sounds — TV, radio, the web, billboards — bombard us everywhere we go.

But attempting to use the media for our campaign work is like picking up a double-edged sword: the media can both support and destroy good campaigns. It should be approached with caution and also with a good understanding of what you want out of the relationship. This section can help you identify what you want from the media and why and suggests some strategies for success in getting your message out to as wide an audience as possible.

Group Aims

Think about what you want to get out of using the media. Discuss it in your group and be clear about your aims, which could be to:

- Gain new members/participants for action or event.
- Apply critical pressure on a specific issue through showing widespread opposition.
- Make more visible an issue or way of working that you criticise.
- Send messages to your opponents.

INDYMEDIA PRESS CENTRE IN GOTHENBURG, SWEDEN.   PHOTO: SIMO HELLSTEN

Messaging

Spend time as a group working out your 'key messages'. Preferably, you will not have more than three for one action or campaign. Define them as carefully and concisely as possible. Write them down and make sure everyone in your group knows what they are and is happy or at least can live with them. Remember: these are your public messages, so write them in clear and easily digestible language that everyone (both in and outside of your group) can understand.

Think about how your target group(s) might receive these key messages. Can the messages be changed to be more attractive and still stay on focus? Defining and agreeing upon your messages is useful because it can enable and empower more people in your group to communicate with the media. It will make your communications more consistent, reinforce your position, and keep you focused. Make sure that all your communications with the media include one or more of these key messages. Role play encounters with journalists to practice your key messages and how to interact with the media in an effective way (see 'Role Play' Exercise, p134).

Types of Communication

There are many different ways of engaging with the media. Common for all the different ways presented below is the importance of thinking like a journalist. Ask yourself: What is newsworthy? What is interesting for others to read? What is the news? At the same time keep your focus on your key messages!

Note that media in different countries function differently. Find out how it works in your country and make appropriate changes. Ask a journalist or an activist with media experience in your country to give you hints about what to think about.

Press Releases

A good press release will get picked up. Try to piggy-back on bigger news stories if you can relate them to your campaign activity. For example, if a government or celebrity makes a statement about your general field, write a short press release the same day with your group's response. You can also use this opportunity to flag an event or action you have planned or a particular campaign strand you have underway (example: a petition you are running). Write clearly and concisely, give your piece a snappy, topical, and clever headline, and know how to get it to journalists (maintain an email/fax/phone database). Always include the date and contact details for a spokesperson or media contact from your group. Target press releases to local and thematical press. For example: 'Woman from Oxford arrested in nuclear weapons protest' to an Oxford paper or 'Swedish priest arrested in nuclear weapons protest' to a Swedish Church/Christian paper. Your group's media person should collect information for the targeted press releases from everyone in the action group: e.g., name (correct spelling), age, occupation, origin, quote about the action. If quotes, facts, and background are included in a press release, you have done much of the journalistic work and media can easily publish it.

Spokesperson/Designated Media Person

Make sure you always have an identifiable contact point for the media. Get that group member an email address and a mobile phone. Make sure she or he is always well-briefed and can watch the media for developments in your field so as to respond adequately to new information. If there is a risk of arrest, the media person should be non-arrestable in order to be accessible for the media while others are arrested. Ideally you should have more than one media person.

Meeting Journalists

Building good relationships with individual journalists is possible. Remember, if they are interested in your issue, you will probably get results if you help by supplying good quality, accurate information and doing them the odd favour, such as giving them key information that you have not given to other journalists. After all, most journalists love a scoop. However, be careful too: some journalists will misquote and misrepresent you (deliberately or otherwise). This is most likely with tabloid press and more right-wing press, but not exclusively.

Agencies

Make sure your press releases are sent to national and international press agencies. Sometimes stories not picked up by media outlets you have contacted directly are picked up later because the story appears on the wires. Call agencies and media after you have sent a press release. Ask if they have received the press release and if they will do a piece on it. Make sure they know who you are and how you can be contacted if they want more information later.

Letters Page

One good way to communicate your messages to the general public is to have one or two people in your group who buy the main newspapers every day and who then write letters about the content of the papers which relates to their field. You can get a lot of letters published this way, especially with local/regional media. Such visibility helps to make your campaign seem bigger, stronger, and more engaged than it may actually be. Don't always have the same people write the letters — after a while the editors will notice!

Website

Your Website is an important tool for communicating your messages; journalists will visit it for background. Make sure your site is always updated. Consider creating a separate section — a 'media centre' — for your press releases, with high quality images (which you own and do not mind others using or reprinting) and succinct background information. Obviously, it should also include direct contact details for your media person (phone, email). A blog (a website written by individual members or the group) is a new way to spread information about an action. Don't write things that you don't want to media to print, if you want to use the blog for the media or it is public.

Writing for/Engaging with Alternative Media

Alternative media in its many forms can be your friend in gaining support. But it is not generally read or viewed by a huge audience. And you will probably have to do a lot of the writing yourself! Sites in the global indymedia network can help you communicate about your campaign to a generally sympathetic audience, but this is unlikely to 'apply critical pressure' or 'mainstream an unpopular issue/way of working'. It may however, gain you a few new activists and, in some cases send messages to your opponents (the police and some companies are monitoring bits of the alternative media around the clock). The alternative media can also provide a space for disparate campaigns to identify opportunities for working together and to explore ideas about what works and what doesn't based on collective experience.

Planning a Media Campaign

So, we have some idea of the practical methods of communicating our messages, but to get the most out of your effort, invest some time planning a 'media campaign'. This means figuring out how to communicate both effectively and strategically and with the consent of the rest of the group. Media campaigns are best suited for short-term projects or by breaking down your campaign into bite-sized pieces. To get the most from this process, you must integrate your media campaign into a complete campaign strategy and define your key messages clearly (see 'Messaging', p50).

For example, imagine a group which aims to expose and undermine a particular arms company. Say the group is planning to work for the next six months to get some of the company's suppliers to stop working with them. The group may be considering writing to those suppliers, lobbying their workers, blockading their depots, and so on. A good media campaign should be able to sell the group's activities as positive — and and the company's as negative. First, consider the obvious criticisms of your group's strategy. For example: 'the trade is legal', 'you are disrupting ordinary workers', or 'your tactics are threatening'. Before you ever send a single press release, work out responses to such criticisms. One way to do this is to prepare a basic 'question and answer' sheet for any group members who will be dealing with the media. This briefing sheet should include your key messages at the top.

If the campaign has key events over the six-month period, plot these out and work out what information you should send to the media and when. Consider sending advance notice of events a couple of weeks beforehand and more detailed/confirmed information three of four days before (or at a time that meets local media deadlines — for example, in Britain, most weekly newspapers go to press on Thursday, so send information on Tuesday night/Wednesday morning). Send information about what happened at the event on the day itself. Plot these releases out over the six months of the campaign. Likewise, if there are key government or industry events, reports being released, international bodies meeting, etc., plot these dates and work out how you can respond to them. Be prepared! Make sure you have a decent number of high-resolution images that sell your campaign. Take good photos at events and actions and make them available to journalists on request or for download from your Website.

Work out which media are likely to be sympathetic to the campaign and its tactics but also have a big and broad readership. Invest energy in cultivating your relationship with these. Regional media (press, radio, TV) are often keen for content and are more likely to publish/broadcast you. Make sure you include the local/regional media in any communications.

Summary of General Tips

Try to build good relationships with journalists; you can help each other. But remember: journalists can't always be trusted. Always release to agencies, as you never know where in the world something will be picked up. Always have a group member on hand to deal with media enquiries. Keep press releases short and simple. Be prepared for tough questions. Stay on message. Go for local angles. Ask other campaigners, share knowledge, read manuals, or attend free or low-cost training courses.

FOOD NOT BOMBS ACTION IN MOSCOW, RUSSIA. PHOTO: ANDREAS SPECK

Campaign Case Study Guide

It is important to document campaigns so people can learn from them. Just as we have learned from the nonviolent campaigns of people throughout time and around the world, documenting our own struggles and stories may help people in other times and places. This guide, created for WRI's Nonviolent Social Empowerment case studies, can be used by an individual or group to determine the information needed to construct a case study of a campaign. This guide can also be used to remind us of what we need to consider in organising a campaign.

Overview

- Nature of the campaign/movement: What was/is the issue? When did it start/finish?
- Geographical and (brief) historical context
- Participants: Who (analysis of class, race/ethnic, gender, religious group, age, sexuality, ability, other) did this change at different phases of the movement?

Chronology

- Starting point
- Were there (have there been) distinct phases?
- Were there particular moments of expansion?
- What were the peaks?
- What were other key events?

Nonviolence

- Was there a public profile of wanting to avoid violence?
- Was this issue raised? Was there any decision how?
- Was there a declared public policy of nonviolence?
- If so, what was meant by nonviolence?
- Was there consensus around this? What kind of diversity was there around this?
- What measures were taken to implement a policy of nonviolence?
- Was the campaign seen as shifting the values of society more towards nonviolence?
- Were there particular sources of inspiration for types of action or ways of organising?

Means

- What use was made of official channels, lobbying, electoral processes, or constitutional mechanisms, and with what impact?
- How did you try to use mainstream media?
- What role or influence did it have?
- How did you try to develop or use your own public media or alternative

media? With what impact?

- Did your movement try to establish alternatives? What happened?
- What kind of means did you use to build a movement culture or sense of connectedness? To what effect?
- Did you use withdrawal of cooperation as a tactic? At what stage? With what effect?
- Did you try to directly disrupt or obstruct an activity you were campaigning against? At what stage? With what focus? With what participation? With what effect?
- How did you use conventional means of protest? How did you combine them with other methods?

Organisation

- Did the campaign/movement agree on a formal structure?
- What informal structures played an important role?
- Was the campaign/movement concerned with having a participatory structure of organisation and decision-making?
- How did the campaign/movement link with other groups/movements?
- What importance did it give to coalition-building? With what criteria for alliances?
- How did the movement address the needs of activists to learn, to grow, to rest, to sustain their commitment?
- How did the movement address the possible contradiction between the needs of security and the desire for participation?
- What kind of repression did the movement expect to face? What provision did it make to support the people most affected?
- Did the movement have a clear timeframe and concept of strategic development?
- How did the movement develop its resources (human, social, economic)?

Goals and Outcomes

- What were the campaign/movement's initial goals?
- How has its goals evolved? Why?
- Was it an aim to empower participants? In what way?
- How were the goals framed, e.g., with what type of slogan?
- Did the campaign/movement have the flexibility to revise goals, e.g., to respond to particular events or to build on success?
- How did the campaign/movement expect change from the institution holding power or those who 'benefit' from being dominant (e.g., to be converted, to accommodate some demands, to be coerced into accepting demands, to disintegrate/dissolve)?
- To what extent were short-, medium-, and long-term goals achieved?
- What were side effects(both positive and negative)?
- Did the adversary make any mistakes that significantly helped the campaign/movement's cause?

Empowerment

All the previous questions have some link with empowerment, but this concluding section returns to this theme with more focus. Answers need to encompass the dimensions of power within, power-with, and power-in-relation to.

- Who was empowered? to be or do what (to join in, to share responsibility, to take initiative, to maintain their activism)?
- What contributed to this sense of empowerment (e.g., training, group confidence, achieving strategic goals)?
- How did the experience of different phases of a movement affect the sense of empowerment?
- What about people involved who did not feel empowered? Why didn't they (due to external or internal factors)?
- How were strategies of empowerment discussed or constructed on the personal, group, and social levels?
- Was any participant/group disempowered and how? How did this affect the campaign?

6

ORGANISING FOR EFFECTIVE NONVIOLENT ACTIONS

Sending the Protest Message — Making an Action Effective

Jørgen Johansen and Brian Martin

What makes a protest action effective? Organisers have lots of potential choices: what, when, where, how, and who. Looking at how audiences are likely to respond to messages can give you guidance.

Heads of government are coming to town. Let's organise a protest! We'll have a massive rally and march. Those who want can blockade the venue. We'll make our concerns about inequality, exploitation, and aggression known far and wide.

But wait a second. Will this sort of protest be effective? Is it going to change people's viewpoints, mobilise support, and help bring about a better society? Or, instead, will it enforce prejudices, alienate potential supporters, and suck energy away from more effective initiatives? And anyway what does it mean to 'be effective'?

These questions have no simple answers. Actions have many different impacts. Many are hard to measure and some are entirely overlooked. Weighing the pros and cons is difficult: it's an emotional as well as a rational matter.

Context

Actions need to be designed with the context in mind. What is appropriate in one situation could be completely counterproductive in another. Laws, media, police, culture, religion, civil society, and many other factors are very different in Burkina Faso, Germany, Nepal, Indonesia, and China.

In India in 1930, Gandhi chose to build a campaign around salt, a potent symbol for Indians because of the British salt laws. What could protesters use as a

DEMONSTRATION IN QUITO, ECUADOR. · PHOTO: ACCIÓN ECOLÓGICA ECUADOR

potent symbol in Swaziland or Sweden today? Actions must be designed with a deep knowledge of the local conditions. As a general rule, success stories should never be copied, but they can function as inspirations and as useful cases from which to learn.

Open-ended hunger strikes are regarded very differently in a Christian culture than in a Hindu society. For atheists and Christians sacrificing your life means a lot, whereas a Hindi anticipates thousands more lives to come — an important difference! In a country where an activist risks torture, lengthy imprisonment, or the death penalty, civil disobedience is a different matter than where the likely outcome is a fine or a few weeks in a decent prison. It is wise for activists to act differently in countries with strict censorship and state-run media than where free and oppositional media regularly cover demonstrations.

Choices

There are two main types of actions: (1) oppose and (2) promote. The first focuses on what organisers disagree with and the second on the alternative organisers are offering. Within each of these are many options. In most cases, it's much easier to create a positive image when an alternative can be constructed. To say 'no'! is common and easy but will often be regarded as unhelpful or as blocking progress. To present alternatives is more demanding but often rewarded by being seen as constructive.

Within each of these main categories there is again a choice: direct action or indirect action. Direct action means activists themselves doing something about the problem/conflict. It could be to close a city street to change it into a space for pedestrians. Or it could be to squat in a house and turn it into a cultural centre. When activists in Genetix Snowball destroy genetically modified plants from fields in Britain, they are not only demanding that these fields should be made illegal but are removing the plants themselves. These types of actions are often illegal and risky. The point is that the activists themselves are making the change directly: they are taking direct action. Indirect actions involve asking someone else, such as politicians or business executives, to respond to a demand or deal with an unjust situation. Note that in a dictatorship, making requests can be a form of direct action, because it is an exercise of free speech.

For both direct and indirect actions there is a need to develop more types of actions. Creativity, fantasy, and experiments are crucial. Just as arms producers come up with more sophisticated weapons every year, activists need to develop new forms of action. Good examples should be tested, documented, and adapted for use at other times, places, and circumstances.

Nonviolent Action

DIRECT ACTION CAN BE LEGAL OR ILLEGAL (CIVIL DISOBEDIENCE), AND CIVIL DISOBEDIENCE CAN BE EITHER SYMBOLIC/INDIRECT OR DIRECT ACTION.
IMAGE: WAR RESISTERS LEAGUE'S ORGANIZER'S MANUAL BY ED HEDEMANN

Audiences

On many issues there are three main groups: activists, opponents, and third parties. When a group wants to challenge a repressive government, the activists are those involved in protests. The opponents are the government and its agencies, such as the police and the army. The third parties are those not directly involved in the struggle: the general public and most people in other countries. People can move from being a third party to being an activist, and the other way around, as a consequence of actions. One goal is to engage more people. In most cases the media are carriers of information/propaganda and messages from the event to wider audiences.

 For analysing where people stand, see 'Spectrum of Allies' Exercise, p130; for more on the media, see 'The Role of the Media', p49.

Alignment Between Methods/Medium and Audience

As well as looking at who the audiences are, it's helpful to look at the interaction between activist methods and audiences. Media guru Marshall McLuhan said 'The medium is the message'. For example, television encourages a certain way of viewing the world, irrespective of what's on the screen. Personal conversation encourages a different perspective.

In activism, too, the medium — namely the method of action — is the message. According to a perspective in psychology called correspondent inference theory, audiences make assumptions about someone's motivations according to the consequences of their actions. When activists threaten or use violence-for example, bombings, assassinations, or hijackings — many observers believe the goal of the activists is to destroy society. The method, namely destruction, is assumed to reflect the goal. For example, after 9/11, many people in the United States thought al Qaeda's goal was to destroy U.S. society. This was the wrong message. Very few U.S. citizens knew that Osama bin Laden's key goals concerned U.S. government policies in the Muslim world.

The same thing applies on a much smaller scale. If a worker on a picket-line spits on a manager, the message is one of contempt and disrespect, which can distract audiences from the message that the pay is too low or working conditions are unsafe.

Actions are more powerful when the method used — the medium — aligns with the message. In the U.S. civil rights movement, well-dressed blacks entered white-only restaurants and sat politely and quietly at lunch counters, not responding to abuse and police provocation. Their presence and respectful demeanour sent a powerful message that was aligned with their short-term goal (equal access to the restaurant), as well as the long-term goal of racial equality. On the other hand, the abuse by white patrons and aggressive action by police, directed only at blacks in the restaurant, sent the message that segregation was a system of racism, exclusion, and aggression. These powerful messages helped discredit segregation among audiences in the rest of the United States and the world.

Dealing with Attack

Protesters often come under attack: they may be slandered, harassed, beaten, arrested, imprisoned, even killed. Their communications may be intercepted, their offices raided, and their equipment confiscated or destroyed. These attacks are hurtful and expensive, damaging to morale, and can discourage participation. But with the right preparation and tactics, and good luck, some attacks can be made to backfire on the attackers. It's not easy and doesn't happen often, but it can be very powerful.

Perpetrators and their supporters regularly use five methods to inhibit outrage from their attacks:

- cover up the attack
- devalue the target
- reinterpret what happened (including lying, minimising effects, and blaming others)
- use official channels to give an appearance of justice
- intimidate and bribe targets and their supporters.

For example, after police assault protesters, the police and their supporters may use every one of these five methods.

- Police, in assaulting protesters, often try to do it away from witnesses and cameras.
- Police, politicians, and commentators denigrate protesters as being unprincipled, foul-mouthed, ill-behaved brats, rent-a-crowd (professional protesters), thugs, scum, criminals, or terrorists.
- They claim that police were doing their duty, that protesters were violent and disturbing the peace, and indeed that it was the police who came under attack.
- When protesters make formal complaints or go to court, seldom are there any serious consequences for abusive police. Meanwhile, the whole process takes so long that most people lose interest while activists are tied up in technicalities and distracted from activism.
- In many cases protesters don't speak out for fear of police reprisals; in a court action they may accept a settlement to resolve the matter, often with a silencing clause attached.

Each of the five methods can be challenged.

✱ *For more information about how to deal with the psychological conseque-nces, see 'Coping with the Stress and Strain of Taking a Stand', p63.*

Conclusion

In deciding on what, when, and how to protest, it's useful to think of audiences and messages.

Context

Actions need to be designed with the context in mind. What is appropriate in one situation could be completely counterproductive in another.

Choices

There are two main types of actions: (1) oppose and (2) promote. The first focuses on what disagreeing with an action/policy/etc. and the other on an alternative.

Audiences

How do audiences and activist methods interact? Opponents, third parties, and activists themselves are important audiences.

Alignment

How do activist methods align with activist goals? If there is close alignment, the right message will more likely be received.

Attacks

How will an attack be perceived? It's vital to be prepared to counter the methods of cover-up, devaluation, reinterpretation, official channels, intimidation, and bribery.

Postscript: documentation, evaluation and dissemination

For actions to become more effective, activists need to learn from past experiences. They need to document and evaluate what they are doing and make this information available for others. (See 'Action Evaluation', p90.) Just as students at war colleges learn about historical battles from lectures and textbooks, activists must build a similar system for coming generations to learn from the history of social movements. This requires serious, critical evaluations of planning, actions, and outcomes. It is just as important to study mistakes as to celebrate victories. These evaluations must be made available for other activists, taking into account different languages and contexts. It is a large task. There are many actions from which to learn!

> **✱** *This is a shorter version of an article published in* Gandhi Marg, *Vol. 29, No. 4, January-March 2008, pp. 503-519. You can access the full article at: http://www.uow.edu.au/arts/sts/bmartin/pubs/08gm.html*

NONVIOLENT ACTION IN SANTIAGO, CHILE   PHOTO: ARCHIVES OF ROBERTA BACIC

Coping with the Stress and Strain of Taking a Stand

Roberta Bacic with thanks to Clem McCartney

People protest for many reasons, but often it is because we are confronted with a situation to which we must respond and take a stand. The reality we face — be that our own or that of others — pushes us to act, react, challenge, or change what we experience and see. We forget to seriously consider the possible consequences of any such choice. Positive consequences are often empowering. Negative consequences can be disempowering. We need to think about both in advance to prepare for the next steps, but also so we are not surprised by them and suffer even more stress.

Consequences of Taking a Stand

In taking a stand, we may put ourselves into situations that will push us to our limits and put ourselves at risk. If this happens, negative experiences will almost be inevitable; fear will most likely surface as a response. In situations of insecurity and anguish, those feelings will merge: fear of being arrested, fear of being denounced, fear of being tortured, fear of being caught in an illegal meeting, fear of being betrayed, fear of again not achieving our goal, fear of the unknown (what happens if I am arrested?) and also of the known, be it a

63

specific threat by phone or being aware of what has happened to others. We need to know what can be done to avoid those consequences or to cope with them when they arise. Three main elements can help us to function: confidence and solidarity with our fellow protesters, good training, and emotional preparation and debriefing.

Some of the Consequences We Need to Prepare For

1. Dealing with the Consequences of Fear

When we think of traumatic consequences, we immediately think of the physical consequences, such as being manhandled, arrested, beaten, or having our human rights violated. This risk is greater in some societies than others; people protesting in very militaristic and authoritarian states are particularly courageous. But all of us will normally feel at least some anxiety and fear and at least be aware of the risk of physical pain or discomfort. These fears may immobilise us. But ignoring them is not good. If we are not prepared, our natural reactions in the situation may actually lead to greater hurt. For example, we may have an urge to run, but if we start running, we lose our discipline; those opposing us may be tempted to attack at that moment. Being prepared, rationally, emotionally, and practically, is therefore important. Training in fear control is very helpful. (See 'Consequences of Fear' Exercise, p129.)

2. The Strength of Coming Out in Public

We need to be aware that we are choosing to stand outside conventional opinion. It is not so difficult to share our feelings in private with those who share our views, although we may worry about being betrayed. Coming out in public is more difficult. We are taking a stand not only against the state but also against common social attitudes. The very reason that we need to protest is to challenge those conventions, but knowing that does not make it easy. We are exposing ourselves. We think of Women in Black in Israel who simply stood as a silent witness to what they could not accept in their society. Now that form of witness has been used in Serbia, Colombia, and elsewhere. Solidarity with our colleagues is very important in such situations, as is creating space to air and deal with our feelings. Even those who appear confident may have worries with which they need to acknowledge and deal. (A 'Hassle Line' Exercise, p119, is helpful to practice.)

3. Preparing Ourselves to Deal with Distress

Other risks and consequences may be more subtle, but for that very reason can be more distressing. We may face disrespect and humiliation or be mocked and goaded by bystanders or state forces. Again Women in Black come to mind; they were spat at and abused by a hostile public, yet remained silent and non-reactive. This can be emotionally distressing. Role playing (see Exercise, p134) a situation in advance helps us to prepare emotionally and to understand more fully the motivations (and fear) of our opponents. Solidarity and confidence in our fellow protesters is again important and is partly built up by such rehearsals. Less emotionally distressing, because it is less immediate, is bad publicity. The press, who may libel us with all kinds of inaccuracies, may challenge our good faith and motivations. Preparing ourselves for such humiliation makes it easier to cope with it when it comes.

4. Putting Yourself in the Position of the Other

We may even seek out humiliation as part of the statement we are trying to make, as when protesters try to put themselves into the situation of people they are defending. Many groups have done street theatre playing the parts of prisoners and guards at Guantánamo Bay; unanticipated feelings rose to the surface, which participants sometimes found difficult to control. For instance, the 'prisoners' may begin to feel violated while the 'guards' find themselves either entering into the experience too enthusiastically or feeling a sense of revulsion. Either way, participants may feel defiled and polluted. To deal with such possibilities they need to be prepared for such reactions in themselves and be debriefed sensitively afterwards. Another example is protests over factory farming when volunteers use their own bodies to model slabs of meat. The reaction may be to feel really enthusiastic and liberated by taking a stand or alternatively troubled at the situation they have put themselves into.

5. Dealing with Disillusionment

Sometimes we have few problems before and during the protest, but a real blow comes later if we seem to have had no impact. The huge protests against the war in Iraq on 15 February 2003 did not stop the war. Our worst fears were realised. Not surprisingly, many people were disillusioned and disempowered. Naturally they asked, 'Was it worth doing'? They may not want to take part in the future in other actions on this or other issues, feeling it worthless. What can be done to address this disillusionment? We need opportunities to reflect together on what has happened and what we can learn from the experience (See 'Action Evaluation', p90.) We need to adjust our expectations. Protests are important to show our strength, but they alone will not stop a war.

6. Dealing with Success

As well as worrying that a situation may turn out worse than anticipated, we might have, paradoxically, difficulty coping with what might on the surface seem positive or successful. Examples are if security forces act more humanely than we anticipated or authorities engage with us and seem willing to consider our demands. Such outcomes can have an unsettling effect if we have steeled ourselves for confrontation. What happens to all the adrenaline that has been built up in our bodies? What do these developments do to our analysis? Are we wrong in our analysis? Should we trust the system more? Or are we being duped by sweet words? Our movement may achieve more solidarity when we are faced with harsh opposition and may fracture when that does not materialise.

Organising

Therefore, we need to be ready to know what responses might be most effective and test out what is possible. Then, when and if it happens, we are more able to collectively assess the situation and act appropriately.

7. When Levels of Aggression Rise

Many of us have been shocked at the aggression that arises during a nonviolent protest — and not only from those opposed to the protest. We may find a wave of aggression rising in ourselves when we are treated roughly by authorities. Even if we do not react, such a feeling can make us very uncomfortable and doubtful. Or other protesters may start to riot, and we have to be able to find an appropriate response. Do we join in, leave, or hold our ground, continuing the protest nonviolently as planned? Such situations leave little time to think, so possibilities need to be considered in advance. We need to have our clear alternatives so that quiet decisions can be made. (See 'Decision-Making' and 'Role Playing' Exercises p133 and p134.)

Different Contexts

In the North, we might protest in states and cultures that claim to be liberal and democratic. Or we might be in an authoritarian regime. But we should not assume that protest is easier in liberal democracies, as some such states can be very harsh in their treatment of protest.

Other factors may determine the potential of protest and its limits. The society may be closed or open. In a closed society the risks are greater because dissidents can disappear, and there is little possibility of any accountability. It may have a functioning judicial system, independent of the government, that can act as a check on human rights abuses. The culture of a society is also a significant factor as it may value conformity and respect for authority. Or a society may feel weak and vulnerable to the pressures of modernity or the influence of other states; in such situations, any form of protest may be seen as disloyal and destructive.

While protest is more difficult in some situations than others, all the issues discussed here may arise in any context, albeit with varying intensity.

✱ *For more on contexts, see also 'Sending the Protest Message', p57.*

Conclusion

If we prepare for the mixture of emotions and reactions that may result from our protest, build solidarity with our colleagues, and analyse and debrief ourselves on the consequences of our actions, then we are better placed to continue the struggle for a better society, even though we may know that that will not be achieved in our lifetime, if at all.

However, if we do not prepare well and deal well with the consequences, we may end up not helping anyone, even ourselves. We may get discouraged and decide to give up or take up other types of strategies that may be counter-productive, such as mainstream politics and the use of force. Or we may get into a pattern of protesting for its own sake, without any strategic sense. As such, we may appear superficially to be still engaged in the struggle and others may admire our persistence, but we have lost a purpose for all the energy we expend. Our ineffectiveness and purposefulness may discourage others from engaging. If — as I believe — we have a duty to protest, we also have a duty to prepare ourselves well: to identify the risks to our physical and emotional well-being and to take steps to ensure that we can overcome these risks and continue the struggle in a positive and effective manner, keeping true to our ideals. Last, but not least, let's keep trying, have some fun while we do it, and by that, give peace a chance. We are not the first ones to do it, nor will be the last ones.

Humour and Nonviolent Actions

Majken Sorensen

We usually use nonviolent action about serious problems. Thinking about an action in humorous terms may therefore seem a strange way to deal with an issue and not your first choice. However, humour and seriousness may be much more closely related than at first they appear. Almost all good humour thrives on contradictions and absurdity; nonviolent action often tries to point out the contradiction between the world as it is and the world as we want it to be. Humour is powerful because it turns the world as we know it upside down and escapes the logic and reasoning that is an inevitable part of the rest of our lives.

How to Start?

If humour doesn't come to you easily, don't despair — it can be learned. Watch your opponent: If there is a contradiction between what they say and what they do, might this be the basis for a good joke? The closer you stick to the truth about what your opponent is saying and doing, the better the humour will work. Almost all dictators say that what they are doing is 'for the good of the people'. That kind of statement might be contradicted by their actions.

Using Humour Wisely

- Don't overdo it — humour should be used with moderation and works best if complemented with a serious message.
- Choose the object of your humour carefully!

CLOWNING AROUND DURING FREEDOM TO PROTEST DEMONSTRATION, LONDON, UK.   PHOTO: IPPY

If you are making a political action, you want a political message, and you want to stick to the point. How people look, their ways of speaking, or their sexuality are not good subjects. Making jokes about such things is usually not the way to reach out to other people and also takes attention away from the political point you want to make. At the end of this section are two examples of actions that stick to the political points and don't get sidetracked.

Why Use Humour?

Using humour in your actions can be useful in a number of ways. First, it should be fun for those who participate in the action. Humour has a potential to prevent and counter activist burnout, although it is not a magic solution.

Using humour is also a way to increase the chance of getting attention from media, potential supporters, and bystanders. Journalists who know that they will get good images and a lively story are more likely to show up when you announce that something is going to happen.

If you are part of a small movement that wants to expand, humour will show potential members that although you work on a serious issue, you are still capable of enjoying life.

The Power of Humour

Humour is a powerful way to relate to your opponent, as the 'absurdity' of your actions will change both the relationship and the logic of rational argumentation. Both the police and the opponent may have difficulty responding to good, humorous actions. They can provide a perfect opportunity for creating a 'dilemma action', meaning that no matter what your opponents do, they have lost and are likely to appear weaker in the eyes of both bystanders and the people on 'their' side. But be prepared for harsh reactions if you humiliate anybody. When you make it difficult for your opponents to find an 'appropriate' reaction (adequate from their point of view), frustration might cause a violent reaction.

Examples of Humorous Actions

Two examples can illustrate some of the points above. We don't recommend that you copy them directly, as your context is likely to be very different. But they can show how powerful humour can be:

In Norway in 1983, a small group of total objectors organised in the group 'Campaign against Conscription', (KMV in Norwegian) refused both military and alternative service. They wanted to create public debate and change the law that gave them 16 months in prison. The state refused to call it 'prison' and instead said the objectors would 'serve their service in an institution under the administration of the prison authorities'. To avoid having political prisoners, there were officially no trials, no prisoners, and no punishment. The cases of the total objectors went through the courts only to identify the objector, and the result was always the same: 16 months in prison. Sometimes the prosecutor never showed up because the result was clear anyway. KMV exploited this in one of their actions:

One of the activists dressed up as the prosecutor and overplayed his role, demanding that the total objector get an even longer prison term because of his profession (he was a lawyer). During the procedure in the court, nobody noticed anything wrong in spite of the 'prosecutor's' exaggerations. One week later KMV sent their secret video recording of the case to the media, with the result leaving most of the Norwegian public laughing.

This example clearly illustrates the power of turning things upside down. A friend of the accused playing the prosecutor and demanding a stronger punishment than what the law can give parodies the court. In this action, KMV activists satirised the absurdity of having a court case with nothing to discuss; they succeeded in getting attention from both media and 'ordinary people'. In addition to turning the roles upside down, the parody of the court also exposed the contradiction between what the Norwegian state said and what it did. If the politicians call Norway a democracy and claim that it has no political prisoners, why are people sent to prison for their beliefs? And why is that imprisonment not even called a prison sentence, but an administrative term for serving alternative service? This is an absurd situation. Through dramatising it in a humorous frame, KMV cut through all rational explanations and made people understand that this did not make sense.

However, this case also makes the important point that the activist using humour should be aware of the context it is used in. If you want to avoid long prison terms, imitating this kind of action is not recommended.

In a second example, we move from democratic Norway to dictatorial Serbia in the year 2000, before the fall of Slobodan Miloševic. To support agriculture, Miloševic placed boxes in shops and public places and asked people to donate one dinar (Serbian currency) for sowing and planting crops. In response, the youth movement Otpor arranged its own collection called 'Dinar za Smenu'. Smenu in Serbian is a word with many meanings; it can mean change, resignation, dismissal, pension, or purge. This action, consisting of a big barrel with a photo of Miloševic, was repeated several times in different places in Serbia. After donated a dinar, people would get a stick they could use to hit the barrel. On one occasion, a sign suggested that if people did not have any money because of Miloševic's politics, they should bang the barrel twice. When the police removed the barrel, an Otpor press release said that the police had arrested the barrel and that the action was a huge success. They claimed they had collected enough money for Miloševic's retirement, and that the police would give the money to Miloševic.

This is an example of a dilemma action, because Otpor left both Miloševic and the police with no space for reaction. If the police did not take away the barrel, they lost face. When they did do something, Otpor continued the joke by calling it an arrest of a barrel and saying that the police would give Milošević the money for his retirement. No matter what the regime did, it lost.

✱ *You can find Majken's dissertation on humour and nonviolence on the Website of the Centre for Peace and Reconciliation Studies, Coventry University http://www.coventry.ac.uk/researchnet/external/content/1/c4/ 11/36/v1202125859/user/Humour%20as%20Nonviolent%20Resistance.pdf*

Working in Groups

A challenge for any nonviolent movement is how to prepare its actions. Since the 1976 occupation of the Seabrook nuclear power site, in New Hampshire, USA, (see 'Seabrook-Wyhl-Marckolsheim', p96) a number of Western nonviolent campaigns have favoured using an affinity group model of action coupled with consensus decision-making. This section introduces that style.

Affinity Groups

'Affinity groups' are autonomous groups of 5 to 15 persons. An affinity group in this sense is a group of people who not only have an affinity for each other, but who know each other's strengths and weaknesses and support each other as they participate (or intend to participate) in a nonviolent campaign together. Affinity groups and spokescouncils (see p71) challenge top-down, power-over decision-making and organising and empower those involved to take creative direct action. They allow people to act together in a decentralised and non-hierarchical way by giving decision-making power to the affinity group. Affinity groups have been used constructively in mass anti-globalisation actions in the USA (Seattle 1997), anti-nuclear protests in Europe and North America (beginning in the 1970s), and other large and small nonviolent protest actions in many countries.

With Whom Does One Create an Affinity Group?

The simple answer is: with people you know and who have similar opinions about the issue(s) in question and the methods of action to use to address it. They could be people you meet at an educational seminar, work with, socialise with, or live with. The point to stress, however, is that you have something in common other than the issue bringing you together and that you have mutual trust.

An important aspect of being part of an affinity group is to learn each other's standpoints regarding the campaign or issue and your preferred methods of action. This can involve sharing time together, discussing the issues and methods of action, or doing some form of activist-related training together (like attending a workshop) or working out how to deal with an opponent's or the police's tactics (e.g., counter-demonstrations, misinformation campaigns, agents provocateurs). You should develop a shared idea of what you want individually and collectively from the action/campaign, how it will conceivably go, what support you will need from others, and what you can offer others. It helps if you have agreement on certain basic things about the action: how active, how spiritual, how nonviolent, how deep a relationship, how willing to risk arrest, when you might want to bail-out, your overall political perspective, your action methods, etc.

Group Process

Working in groups, whether in our own families, at workshops, or in continuing organisations, is one of the most basic social activities and is a large part of work for social change. Therefore, it is important that groups working for change develop effective, satisfying, democratic methods of doing necessary tasks, both for their own use and to share with others.

Eliminating authoritarian and hierarchical structures is a form of democratising groups, but it does not mean rejecting all structures. A good group needs to facilitate creativity, community, and effectiveness, in a combination that encourages nonviolence to flourish in ourselves and our society. Good group functioning is a product of cooperative structures and the intelligent, responsible participation of the group's members.

Agreements/Ground Rules

Even if it is an informal group and everyone is relaxed, a group agreement about ground rules is wise. A group contract or a set of rules for the workshop or group, to which everyone agrees, is a very useful guide for the process of a group. It can be referred to if difficulties should arise. And it can, of course, be adapted or changed. The group decides what to include. For example, a group might agree to start meetings on time, to encourage equal participation, to make decisions with consensus, to take turns facilitating group work, to have only one person speaking at a time, to speak for yourself only, to respect confidentiality, not to bar any question or treat it as stupid, not to allow put-downs, to only volunteer yourself, etc. Many people are now familiar with these ground rules, so a facilitator might draw up a suggested list that the group can adapt. It is important to have active agreement from everyone in the group to make a 'contract' with each other.

One issue that might require clarification is the meaning of 'confidentiality' for this group. Does it mean not sharing anything from the workshop, or does it mean that broad themes and what was done can be shared but that no quotes are given or attributed directly to anyone, or does it mean only not repeating personal stories of group members? The longer the workshop or the more intense or personal the issue, the less experienced people are in group work, or the more sensitive the topic, the more time you may need to spend on clarifying and agreeing to ground rules. Do remember that if the group's situation changes, it may review the 'contract' and decide change the 'rules'. This is an important difference between rules that are imposed upon a group and rules that a group contracts together to follow of their own free will.

✱ *See also 'Principles of Nonviolence', p30.*

Facilitating Group Meetings

Affinity groups often decide to use facilitators to help the group meet its needs. Members of the group often take turns playing this role. A facilitator accepts responsibility to help the group accomplish a common task, for example, moving through the agenda in the time available and making necessary decisions and plans. A facilitator does not make decisions for the group, but suggests ways that will help the group move forward. He or she works in such a way that allows the others to be aware that they are in charge, that their business is being conducted, and that each person has a role to play.

It is important to emphasise that the facilitator's responsibility is to the group and its work, rather than to the individuals within the group. Furthermore, a person with a high stake in the issues will have more difficulty functioning as a good facilitator.

✱ *For more detailed information about group facilitation, see 'Meeting Facilitation — The No-Magic Method' by Berit Lakey (http://www.reclaiming.org/resources/consensus/blakey.html) and the information in Section Four, 'Tasks and Tools for Organising and Facilitating Trainings' (p27).*

Special Roles in a Group Meeting

Taking turns at the various roles in a group helps individuals experience different facets of the group's behaviour and strengthens an affinity group. In addition to the meeting facilitator (who helps the group through its agenda), other roles support the work of the group. These special roles become very useful if the group is larger or if it wants to pay special attention to improving the group process on specific issues.

■ A co-facilitator to aid the facilitator.
■ A note-taker who records decisions and makes sure everyone has a copy so that they know what decisions the group has taken.
■ A time-keeper to help keep the group informed about how well it is following its time plan and progressing towards completing its agenda.

Other roles may be useful at times, especially if the group has recurring problems. For instance, a 'process watcher' might observe patterns of participation in meetings and have suggestions on improving the dynamics or may raise issues about oppressive behaviour, power games, or discrimination (race, gender, class, age) in the group. A 'vibes watcher' might pay special attention to emotional undercurrents, non-verbal communication (including conflict behaviour), or energy levels in the group, making suggestions about improving the group atmosphere before something becomes a problem.

✱ *Adapted from* Tri-denting It Handbook, *Third edition, available at http://tridentploughshares.org/article1072#p26*

Roles in an Affinity Group During an Action

During a nonviolent action, an affinity group decides which roles the action requires and people choose what they will do. Support roles are vital to an action's success and to the participants' safety. The roles listed in this Handbook (see 'Roles In, Before, and After an Action', p86) are common but shouldn't be regarded as a blueprint for all actions. Different actions will need different roles. Each group should think about tasks it will need and how to ensure they're done early in the planning. Sometimes people can take on more than one role, e.g. a legal observer might also be a first-aider, police liaison, or even media contact. The key is to make sure that all necessary roles are covered, that all understand the extent of their commitments before beginning, and that no one takes on tasks (support or otherwise) that they are unable to carry out. (Source: http://www.scotland4peace.org/Peace%20Education/Handout%20Six%20-%20Roles,%20Safety%20and%20Afinity%20Groups.pdf)

Decision-Making

Within nonviolent movements, and especially during nonviolent (direct) actions, decision-making requires special attention. Nonviolence is more than the absence of violence; it is closely linked to issues of power, to the methods of decision-making. To avoid new forms of dominance within a group, its discussion and decision-making processes need to be participatory and empowering. Consensus decision-making aims to encourage all to participate and express their opinions, trying to find support for decisions in the group by involving all of its members. It is likely that group members will much more strongly support a decision made with the consensus process. Consensus can be used in many different group situations and is especially useful when a group is preparing to carry out nonviolent actions with each other. Some groups adopt a system where first they try to reach consensus, but if they cannot within a reasonable time limit, then they will vote. However, this is not usually necessary in small affinity groups.

Participating in actions at the Women's Peace Camp in Greenham Common in England in the 1980s, the U.S. feminist writer and nonviolence trainer Starhawk found herself in culture shock. 'In contrast to our [U.S.] West coast style of consensus, involving facilitators, agendas, plans, and formal processes, their meetings seemed to have no structure at all. . . . I found a delicious sense of freedom and an electricity in discussions unhampered by formalities. The consensus process I had known and practised seemed, in retrospect, overly controlled and controlling. . . . At the same time, the Greenham-style process also has drawbacks. The group's preference for action rather than talk produces an inherent bias toward more extreme and militant actions. With no facilitation, louder and more vocal women tend to dominate discussions. Women who have fears, concerns or alternative plans often felt unheard. Each group needs to develop a decision-making process that fits its unique circumstances. The balance between planning and spontaneity, between formal processes and informal free-for alls, is always alive, dynamic, and changing. No one way will work for every group' (Starhawk, Truth or Dare : Encounters with Power, Authority and Mystery. [Harper Collins 1987]).

What follows is mainly concerned with consensus decision-making, but it is important to heed Starhawk's warnings about when not to use consensus: a) When there is no group mind (e.g., when members don't value the group's bonding over their individual desires, consensus becomes an exercise in frustration); b) When there are no good choices (e.g., if the group has to choose between being shot and hung); c) When they can see the whites of your eyes ('appointing a temporary leader might be wisest'); d) When the issue is trivial ('flip a coin'); e) When the group has insufficient information.

Consensus Decision-Making is a Process

Consensus is a process for group decision-making by which an entire group of people can come to a common agreement. It is based upon listening and respect and participation by everyone. The goal is to find a decision to which all of the group's members consent; everyone in the group is willing to support the final decision. Be clear, however, that full consent does not necessarily mean that everyone must be completely satisfied with the final outcome: in fact total satisfaction or unanimous agreement is rather rare.

Majority decisions can lead to a power struggle between different factions within a group who compete rather than respect each other's opinions. They use their brilliance to undermine each other. In contrast, the consensus process taps into the creativity, insights, experience, and perspectives of the whole group. The differences between people stimulate deeper inquiry and greater wisdom.

So how does cooperative decision-making work? The opinions, ideas, and reservations of all participants are listened to and discussed. Differing opinions are brought out and noted. No ideas are lost and each member's input is valued as part of the solution. This open and respectful discussion is vital in enabling the group to reach a decision on the basis of which — in nonviolent action — people will put themselves and their bodies 'on the line'.

Consensus can be exciting because the members of the group actively look for ways to create a common agreement. It can also often be difficult, because everyone needs to overcome the attitude that 'my idea is the best solution'. Consensus not only works to achieve better solutions, but also to promote the growth of community and trust within the group. Consensus is an ongoing process and not simply a different method of voting.

Positions Within a Consensus

Since the goal is not a unanimous decision, consensus must have a place for members of the group who do not totally embrace a proposal. Participants in a decision-making process are more willing to support an idea to which they might have some reservations or objections if the group actively accepts and hears their concerns. If a person is given only the choice of support, non-support, or standing aside, it leaves much less room for being part of the consensus.

Within a group consensus five positions might exist:

■ This is a great idea and I support it completely. (Full agreement)
■ I have some reservations, but will support it. (Support)
■ I have serious reservations, but can accept it. (Acceptance)
■ I have objections, but I can live with this. (Tolerance)
■ I cannot do this, but will not stop the group from doing this. (Standing aside)

Of course, if a large number of persons do not support or accept the decision or stand aside, then the consensus is weak and will probably end up with weak results.

In any case, the group should encourage people to express their reservations and objections and should try to address these opinions. This can be done by modifying the proposal or perhaps by offering reassurance or clarification on certain points. At the same time, individuals who do not totally agree with the item under discussion should examine their opinion to see if they could either support, accept, or tolerate the proposed decision or if they might perhaps even stand aside.

It is possible for individual group members to have strong objections or disagreements but at the same time participate in and consent to the decision that a large number of the groups members can support. This is a key awareness and is an important part of coming to consensus. There is a big difference between disagreement with others in the group and blocking consensus. Disagreement is part of the discussion process.

Blocking Consensus

An individual's decision to block a consensus should not be lightly taken. If you block a decision that has strong support by the rest of the group, you are essentially saying to the group that this decision is so seriously wrong that you do not want to permit it to proceed. If, after discussion, the group comes close to a common agreement, but one or more individuals have such a very strong objection that they cannot be part of the consensus, then they have one of the following opinions:

- This is a totally unacceptable or immoral or inhumane decision. I cannot support this in any way, and I cannot allow the group to proceed with this decision. (Blocking)
- I am completely opposed to this and can no longer work together with this group. (Withdrawing from the group)

If a person has strong objections, and especially if she or he decides to block a consensus, it is important to carefully and clearly express the specifics about the objection and the reasons for blocking consensus. In fact, the person should feel obliged to make a better suggestion, one that may be accepted by all. This will help others to understand the objection and may lead to a clarification of the differences. In any case, it is very important that a person review objections and concerns to see if she or he can withdraw the block and just stand aside for this decision, allowing the group to accept the decision.

Minuting a Consensus Decision

After coming to a consensus decision, it can be useful to ask everyone who did not take the position of 'full agreement' to express his/her concerns, reservations, or objections. Recording these concerns, reservations or objections in the minutes, together with the decision itself, demonstrates clearly that the group values the diversity of opinions and encourages everyone to be aware of these concerns in future discussions or follow-up to the decision. Groups that take minority opinions seriously in this way usually enjoy increased cohesiveness in their activities and actions.

If the Group Cannot Come to a Consensual Agreement

If the group cannot come to consensus, maybe the group does not have enough information to make a decision. Perhaps more discussion time is needed? Should the decision be postponed? Does the group want to ask for a new proposal? Would it help for a smaller committee to draw up some alternative proposals?

Important Aspects When Using Consensus

There are many different formats and ways of building consensus, and a wide range of experience shows that it can work. However, a few conditions must be met for consensus building to be possible:

- Common goal or interest: All members of the group need to be united in a common goal or common interest, whether it is an action, living communally, or greening the neighbourhood. It helps to clearly establish what this overall group goal is and to write it down. In situations when consensus seems difficult to achieve, it helps to come back to this common goal and to remember what the group is all about. Consensus requires commitment, patience, and willingness to put the common goal or interest first.
- Commitment to consensus building: The stronger the commitment to using consensus, the better it works. It can be very damaging to a group's process if some individuals want to return to majority voting and are just waiting for the chance to say 'I told you it wouldn't work'.
- Sufficient time: It takes time to learn to work in this way. As a group become more proficient in the process, the time needed for consensus decision-making will decrease. If the group has divergent strong opinions, more time might be needed to reach a consensus.
- Clear process: Make sure that the group is clear about the process it will use for tackling any given issue. Agree beforehand on processes and guidelines. In most cases, this will include having one or more facilitators to help the group move through the process.

Processes for Finding Consensus

- Subjects for discussion need to be well prepared. The issue to be decided should be clearly stated.
- Different opinions need to be openly expressed. Everyone should be given a chance to state his or her opinion or concern.
- Agreed-upon norms may limit the number of times a person asks to speak and or the amount of time a person speaks, to ensure that each participant has a chance to be fully heard.
- Discussions involve active listening and information sharing. Multiple

concerns and information are shared until the sense of the group is clear.
- Dissenters' perspectives are not only listened to but are embraced and actively included in the discussion.
- Differences are resolved by discussion. Facilitators aid this by identifying areas of agreement and pointing out disagreements to encourage deeper discussion.
- Facilitators help the consensus process by articulating the sense of the discussion, by asking if there are other concerns, by asking for polls of the positions in the group, and by proposing a summary of the consensus decision.
- Ideas and solutions are shared with the group and do not belong to an individual. The group as a whole is responsible for the decision, and the decision belongs to the group.

Practical Steps to Reaching Consensus

There are lots of consensus models (see flowchart on p80). The following basic procedure is taken from *Peace News*, a magazine for peace activists, June 1988:

1. The problem, or decision to be made, is defined and named. It helps to do this in a way that separates the problems/questions from personalities.
2. Brainstorm possible solutions. Write them all down, even the crazy ones. Keep the energy up for quick, top-of-the head suggestions.
3. Create space for questions or clarification on the situation.
4. Discuss the options written down. Modify some, eliminate others, and develop a short list. Which are the favourites?
5. State the proposal or choice of proposals so that everybody is clear. (Sometimes it might be useful to break into small sub-groups to write up each proposal clearly and succinctly.)
6. Discuss the pros and cons of each proposal, and make sure everybody has a chance to contribute.
7. If there is a major objection, return to step 6. (This is the time-consuming bit.) Sometimes you may need to return to step 4.
8. If there are no major objections, state the decisions and test for agreement.
9. Acknowledge minor objections and incorporate friendly amendments.
10. Discuss.
11. Check for consensus.

Especially with controversial issues, it may be helpful to take a straw poll of the group's consensus positions at different times during the discussion. A straw poll of consensus positions is just a test of the positions in the group, not the final call for consensus positions. One easy way to do a quick straw poll is ask for a show of hands with 5 fingers showing full agreement, 4 fingers showing support, 3 fingers showing acceptance, 2 fingers showing tolerance, 1 finger showing standing aside, and a fist showing blocking.

Consensus Decision-Making Flowchart

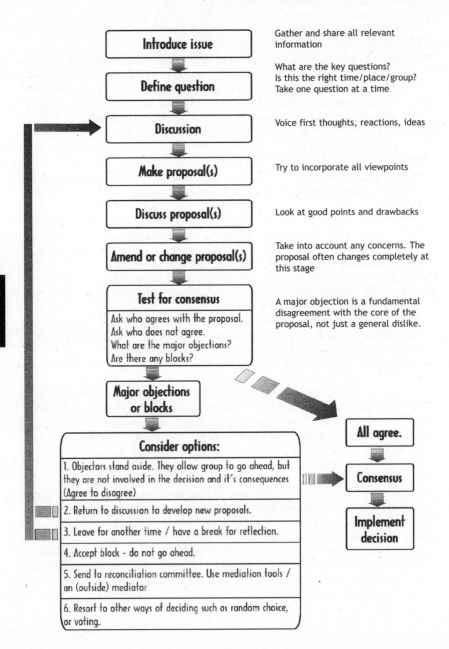

Introduce issue — Gather and share all relevant information

Define question — What are the key questions? Is this the right time/place/group? Take one question at a time

Discussion — Voice first thoughts, reactions, ideas

Make proposal(s) — Try to incorporate all viewpoints

Discuss proposal(s) — Look at good points and drawbacks

Amend or change proposal(s) — Take into account any concerns. The proposal often changes completely at this stage

Test for consensus
Ask who agrees with the proposal.
Ask who does not agree.
What are the major objections?
Are there any blocks?

A major objection is a fundamental disagreement with the core of the proposal, not just a general dislike.

Major objections or blocks

Consider options:

1. Objectors stand aside. They allow group to go ahead, but they are not involved in the decision and it's consequences (Agree to disagree)

2. Return to discussion to develop new proposals.

3. Leave for another time / have a break for reflection.

4. Accept block - do not go ahead.

5. Send to reconciliation committee. Use mediation tools / an (outside) mediator

6. Resort to other ways of deciding such as random choice, or voting.

All agree.

Consensus

Implement decision

For an exercise in practising consensus, see 'Decision-Making', p133.

Consensus in Large Groups: The Spokescouncil

The model of consensus decision-making described above works well within one group. However, bigger nonviolent actions require the cooperation of several affinity groups; one method to do so is to use a spokescouncil. The spokescouncil is a tool for making consensus decisions in large groups. In a spokescouncil, spokespersons from smaller groups come together to make shared decisions. Each group is represented by their 'spoke'. The group communicates to the larger meeting through him or her, allowing hundreds of people to be represented in a smaller group discussion. What the spoke is empowered to do is up to her or his affinity group. Spokes may need to consult with their groups before discussing or agreeing on certain subjects.

Here is an outline process for using the spokescouncil method. (Note: steps 1 and 2 can also take place in advance within the individual small affinity groups.)

1. Whole group (all participants of all affinity groups): Introduce the issue and give all the necessary information.
2. Explain both the consensus and the spokescouncil process.
3. Form small groups (the affinity groups). These could be a random selection of people at the meeting, existing affinity groups, or groups based on where people live or on a shared language.
4. The small groups discuss the issue, gather ideas, discuss pros and cons, and come up with one or more proposals.
5. Each small group selects a spoke (a person from the group who will represent the group's view at the spokescouncil). Small groups decide whether the spoke is a messenger for the group (e.g., relays information between the small group and the spokescouncil) or whether the spoke can make decisions on the group's behalf at the spokescouncil.
6. Spokes from all groups come together in the spokescouncil. They in turn present the view of their small groups. The spokes then have a discussion to try to incorporate the various proposals into one workable idea. During this process, the spokes may need to call time out to refer with their groups for clarification or to see whether a modified proposal would be acceptable to them. The spoke is supposed to speak on behalf of the small group, not to present his or her personal point of view.
7. Once the spokescouncil has come up with one or more possible proposals, the spokes meet with their groups and check for agreement and objections. Groups can also suggest further modifications to the proposals.

Organising

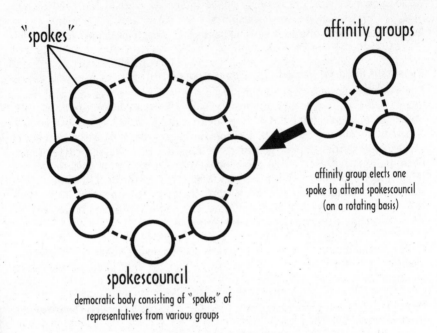

"spokes"

affinity groups

affinity group elects one
spoke to attend spokescouncil
(on a rotating basis)

spokescouncil
democratic body consisting of "spokes" of
representatives from various groups

8. Spokes meet back at the spokescouncil and check whether the groups agree.
   If not all groups agree, the discussion cycle continues, alternating between
   time for the small groups to meet and spokescouncil meetings.
9. Small groups can and often do change their spoke to give different small
   group members the chance to act as spokes for the group.

For an exercise in using a spokescouncil, see 'Decision-Making', p133).

Experiences and Problems

During the past 30 years the model of affinity groups and consensus decision-making has been used in a wide range of small and large-scale nonviolent actions, such as anti-nuclear power actions in the 1970s (Seabrook, New Hampshire, USA; Torness, Scotland), many anti-nuclear energy and disarmament actions in Germany in the 1980s and the 1990s, and anti-globalisation actions in 1999 (Seattle, Washington, USA). Some of the largest actions using the affinity group/spokescouncil/consensus decision-making model have grown to 2000 or more participants (e.g., 1996 in Seabrook, USA, the 1997 protest against nuclear waste transports in Wendland, Germany; see http://www.castor.de/diskus/gruppen/x1000mal/5rundbri.html#Auswertung%20des%20SprechenInnenrates). Many of these experiences point to a changed political environment, especially a growth of decentralised participation in nonviolent actions and campaigns. This has consequences for the way groups now organise for large-scale actions.

Very few affinity groups work long-term. For example, the German anti-nuclear campaign ''X-thousands in the way' has few ongoing affinity groups, though they still exist and form the core of the action. Most activists join the actions of this campaign as individuals or in small groups, forming affinity groups only upon arrival at the action. Therefore, one or two days of preparation are needed before each action to create a community ready and able to act. And even this community is little more than an expanded core of participants. Most activists join spontaneously and without much preparation, and the action has to be planned in a way that makes this possible (Jochen Stay, *Preconditions and Social-Political Factors for Mass Civil Disobedience*, *The Broken Rifle*, No 69, March 2006: http://wri-irg.org/pdf/br69-en.pdf). This structure is more appropriate when one of the aims is to integrate a large number of new activists. The action is generally more low-risk and publicly announced.

Another option is to base larger actions on the autonomy of individual affinity groups, which plan and carry out a variety of small-scale actions simultaneously on their own. The 'large-scale' is then achieved through the number of parallel actions. This structure is more suited to high-risk actions or when a higher level of repression can be expected.

Although the affinity group/spokescouncil structure has been successfully used for various campaigns and actions, it could still be further developed. Groups that do not yet have experience with this structure could practise its use. There is also a need for further experience and evaluation when using it with even larger groups of people.

Check-List for Planning an Action

Preparation for Action

There are times when you will prepare a one-time action, perhaps as your contribution to someone else's campaign, or as a stand-alone event in itself. At other times your action will be part of your wider campaign strategy, with each and every action being a step towards your overall campaign aims. Here we provide a check-list to bear in mind while planning an action.

Before the Action

Framework

■ What is the analysis of the situation?
■ What structure will the group use? Who makes the decisions and how?
■ What is the strategic goal (i.e., who are we trying to influence, and what do we want them to do)?
■ What is the political objective (what is the action or event)?
■ How does this event communicate the group's goals before, during, and after the event?
■ How does the group define its commitment to nonviolence? (Are there non-violence guidelines or stated principles?) (See p30 and p31.)
■ What will the scenario be? (including place and time)
■ Who will provide overall coordination of the event?
■ When and how do you expect the action to end?

> ∗ See 'Developing Effective Strategies' and 'Components of a Campaign' for more ideas and exercises, p34.

Outreach

■ Will the group be trying to work with other groups or communities? If so, what groups and who will make the contacts? (See the 'Spectrum of Allies' exercise, p130.)
■ Will the group have a flyer, explaining to the public what it is doing? If so, who will prepare it?
■ What publicity will you do? Will you try to reach other people to join you? If so, who will do it?
■ What kind of media work will you do? Will you send out a press release ahead of time? Will there be spokespeople during the event, ready to talk to the press? Will there be a media kit with 'talking points'? Will you need a media sub-committee? (See 'The Role of Media', p49.)

Participants' Preparation

- What opportunities do participants in the action have to prepare? Are there orientation sessions? affinity group development? nonviolence training? skills training? legal briefing?
- Are the participants empowered to make decisions about the scenario? How is that done? Is the group process clear to all?
- Is it clear that many roles are needed for an effective action, not just those doing the 'direct action'?

Logistical Preparation

- Are the logistics regarding the time and place well planned?
- Have all the materials been prepared and is there a distribution plan?

During the Action

- Is there a communication system between those in various roles such as police liaison, legal observers, media spokesperson, medical team, people risking arrest, support people, and demonstrators? (See 'Roles In, Before, and After an Action', p86.)
- Who is documenting the action with photographs and video?
- Is the decision-making process clear?

After the Action

- If people were arrested, is there legal and jail support? (See 'Legal Support', p87 and 'Jail Support', p88.)
- Is follow-up media work being done, spreading info on the action to mainstream and alternative media?
- Has the group evaluated the action? (See 'Action Evaluation,' p90.)
- Does the group plan to document the action (creating a case study)? (See 'Campaign Case Study Guide', p54.)
- What are the group's next steps? Will this action lead to the development of a campaign? If part of a campaign, how does it change the situation?

Roles In, Before, and After an Action

Every action requires a range of different tasks, some very visible (e.g., the people blocking a street, the press spokesperson), other less visible, more in the background. Each of these tasks is equally important, as all together make an action possible.

Before an Action
- Coordinator, Campaigner, or Organiser
- Fundraisers
- Research
- Scouting the site or route
- Outreach and organising
- Logistics and support
- Meeting facilitator
- Prop, sign, and banner making, painters, graphic artists, etc.
- Media outreach (ending out media advisory and media releases)
- Media kit preparers
- Writers

During an Action
- People risking arrest (committing civil disobedience)
- Direct support people
- Police liaison
- Peacekeepers/monitors
- Deployment team/diversion
- Media spokesperson
- Media outreach
- Communication team
- Demonstrators/sign-holders/chanters/singers
- Leafletters
- Videographer
- Still photographer
- Medic/EMT/Medical team
- Legal observer(s)
- Jail support contact person

After an Action
- Legal support (See 'Legal Support', p87.)
- Lawyer
- Documentarian/historian/archivist (See 'Campaign Case Study Guide', p54.)
- Fundraisers
- Public speakers
- Letter-writers to decision-makers and newspaper editorial boards

✱ *Adapted from: Rant Collective: www.rantcollective.net*

LEGAL OBSERVER AT PROTEST AGAINST ISRAELI MILITARY TRANSPORTS THROUGH RAF BRIZE NORTON, UK, DURING 2006 LEBANON WAR.   PHOTO: JK

Legal Support

L egal systems are different in every country. However, for actions in which participants will likely be arrested, it is always useful to have a 'legal support team'. This advice on forming such a team in Britain is adapted from the first section of a much longer briefing by the Activist Legal Project at http://www.activistslegalproject.org.uk

Legal support may be in the background of an action, but it is vital. You may be the last home after the action, often spending hours hanging around police stations waiting for activists to be released. You won't share the glamour or get photographed, but without legal support some actions aren't possible. Perhaps if you weren't there, half of those at the 'front-end' of the action wouldn't take part!

The Aims of Legal Support

■ To make sure everyone going on the action is prepared for arrest
■ To liaise with police and solicitors to ensure that arrested activists have appropriate support whilst in custody
■ To ensure that, once released, activists have the emotional and practical support they need

Legal Support Group Roles

The number of people involved in the legal support group will depend upon the size of the action and the number of arrests expected. A number of essential roles have to be fulfilled:

■ Preparing a written legal briefing for the action, including information on arrest procedure, what happens at the police station, likely offences, likely outcomes, bail, and first court hearing
■ Preparing and distributing 'bustcards' to people going on the action (these contain phone numbers in case of arrest)
■ Staffing a phone line (the legal support number), waiting for calls from detainees at police stations
■ Coordination: preparing and updating a definitive list of who has been arrested, including their contacts details, and whether they have been released
■ Police station support: giving support at the police station(s) to arrestees, liaising with solicitors at the police station(s), and meeting detainees on their release from custody
■ Logistics:organising vehicles, drivers, and possibly accommodation to collect and house people released from police custody
■ Organising a defendants' meeting after the action

Unlike legal observers, who do risk arrest by joining activists on the ground, the Legal Support Group should at no stage jeopardise their position with regard to arrest. You are no use to anyone on the inside of a police cell!

＊ *For more information on setting up a legal support for a big mass action, see 'Setting Up a Legal Team' on the U.S.-based Website:*
http://www.midnightspecial.net
For further legal information and workshops contact: Legal Activist Project: info@activistslegalproject.org.uk
http://www.activistslegalproject.org.uk

Movement of Conscientious Objection in the Basque Country (KEM-MOC)

The experience of MOC (Movimiento de Objeción de Conciencia) in helping people in prison is based on the civil disobedience campaign against obligatory military service (the campaign of insumisión, 1971-2002) in which thousands of insumisos were jailed. During this period, various ways of supporting prisoners were suggested and tried. One of the most valued, without a doubt, were the 'support groups'.

SYMBOLIC JAIL ESCAPE. PHOTO: SIMO HELLSTEN

Let's imagine a concrete case to illustrate how these groups function. Bixente Desobediente is an insumiso who will have to serve a sentence of 2 years, 4 months, and 1 day. He needs to convene a meeting with people close to him (family, friends) plus someone from the movement. The first meeting is attended by his girlfriend, his sister, three friends from the neighbourhood, a university pal, a cousin, a guy he met at an anti-militarism discussion group, and a neighbour. This group reviews his decision to be an insumiso, discussing his motives and the consequences it could bring. As not all of those attending understand concepts like civil disobedience, nonviolence, direct action, and antimilitarism, the group looks at these too. In the following meetings, they establish goals. After much brainstorming and discussion, they come up with the following objectives:

Emotional Support

Supporting Bixente emotionally is important during his time before his trial, in court itself, and in prison. One suggestion is hiring a bus so that everybody who wants can go to court and witness the trial. Other suggestions are visiting Bixente in prison and encouraging others to write letters. The idea is that he should not feel alone and should have continual contact with supportive friends. This support should also extend to those close to him, such as his parents.

Organising

Logistical Support

Both before his trial and in prison, Bixente will need material support. Before his trial, he goes into hiding to avoid arrest and pre-trial detention, so people need to bring his things from his previous residence to his current location so that he is not caught. In prison, he needs books and paper to continue his studies. This is also work of the support group.

Political Work

The MOC, the movement to which Bixente belongs, is in charge of the political work. However, the support group can collaborate with this work, joining in protest actions organised by MOC, especially those connected with his trial and imprisonment. At the same time, the support group can reach out politically in the places that Bixente is known (such as his neighbourhood and university) to maximise the benefit provided by the disobedience of Bixente and other prisoners. The support group can also put together an email list to inform people about his case and a Website with information about Bixente's case, antimilitarism, war tax resistance to military spending, peace education, and related links. Every now and then, Bixente can write a letter that can be circulated. The support group should coordinate with the MOC (for instance, having a member attend MOC meetings) and check that its actions are in line with the MOC's overall campaign.

Support groups are a great help, not only for the prisoner, but also for the MOC. They share the work and serve as entry points for people to join the movement. Coordination between the political group, the support group, and with the prisoner is essential. Stable, frequent communication is important. The political criteria come from the political movement, not from the prison; however, visits to the prison by members of both groups is important for developing and coordinating the political work.

Action Evaluation

Evaluation allows us to learn from our experiences. Usually people informally evaluate an event, be it through personal reflections, talking with friends, or meeting with a group of core organisers ('leaders'). What we propose here, however, is a structure for feeding back lessons from an event. Rather than leaving evaluation to chance or confining it to an elite, it should be set up as a planned and collective activity that values the input of people who have played different roles, who bring different kinds of experience, and who have different levels of commitment. Preferably everyone who participated in an action or in organising an event should be encouraged to take part in evaluating it.

When evaluations are a regular part of our work, we have a chance for honest feedback on the process and content of the work and a way to improve in the future. Bear in mind that there will be considerable differences of opinion and that it is not necessary for the group to come to agreement. It is also important to point out what was successful as well as what went wrong, but begin with positive evaluations whenever possible. The structure of the evaluation should be planned carefully.

Some of the most obvious points brought up in an evaluation might be quantitative: we handed out so many leaflets, we attracted so many people, we gained so much media coverage, we blocked a road for so long. If such information is important in evaluating the campaign development, make sure that somebody is monitoring it, that you have a way of counting the number of protesters, that a media group collects information about coverage. However, sometimes the numbers game can distract from the main purpose, especially in the case of repeated protests. Maybe more protesters arrived, but the action made less impact and first-time protesters felt useless, got bored, scared, or in some other way were put off. Maybe a military base entrance was blockaded for a longer time, but the action reached fewer people or was somehow less empowering. Criteria for evaluation need to be linked with the strategic purposes of a particular event.

Below is a check-list to help you in evaluating an action; it can also be used in other areas of your work.

1. Vision, Strategy, and Objectives

■ Was there an overall vision/strategy/objective?
■ Was it relevant to the problem/conflict?
■ Did participants know who initiated the action?
■ Were participants aware of the vision/strategy/objectives?

2. Principles and Discipline

■ Was there a clear discussion and agreement on discipline for the action?
■ Was it followed during the action?
■ Were the planned tactics and those actually carried out consistent with the discipline?
■ Did any of the participants feel that they themselves or others failed to follow the agreed-upon discipline?

3. Preparation and Training

■ Was the preparation/training appropriate?
■ Was the preparation/training adequate?
■ Did it actually aid the participants in coping with the unexpected?
■ Did it meet the needs of those involved?
■ Did it meet the expectations of those involved?
■ Did the necessary community feel developed?

4. Tactics

■ Were the planned tactics adequate?
■ Were the tactics, as planned, actually carried out?
■ Did they meet the needs and expectations of those involved?
■ Were unexpected problems adequately dealt with?
■ Was this done in a way consistent with the discipline/vision/objective?

5. Organisation

■ Did the structure/organisation of the action fit its objective/
strategy/vision/discipline?
■ Was it organised in a democratic way?

6. Impact

A. On the participants

■ Was it relevant?
■ Did it invite/create participation?
■ Did the participants feel in control of the action?
■ Did it increase the initiative and confidence of the participants?

B. On those to whom it was addressed

■ Was it understood?
■ Were objectives reached?
■ Did it close or open options for further action and communication?
■ Were there responses from individuals (opponents) that differed from the
institutions that were a part of it?
■ How did these responses relate to the objectives of the action?

C. On others

■ Did they understand it?
■ Were they alienated by it?
■ Did it have any unexpected results?
■ Were people moved in our direction (neutralised, attracted, catalysed)?

✱ *This evaluation form was developed at the International Seminar on
Training for Nonviolent Action held in Cuernavaca, Mexico, in July 1977.*

7

STORIES AND STRATEGIES

This section is a collection of stories and strategies on the use of nonviolence around the world. Stories help us learn from past experiences; the motivation to act can be influenced by what has been done elsewhere or inspired by the creativity and success of others. Many of the stories describe how people learned strategies from campaigns in other parts of the world or were inspired by contact with activists from other regions. In some occasions the visit of a member of another group was the catalyst; in others, reading materials produced elsewhere or attending an international event led to ideas for campaigns. Additionally, many of the stories explain how campaigns were strengthened through international cooperation.

While the contexts of these stories differ, they all have nonviolence as a common denominator. Some cases focus on education and promoting nonviolence within the activist scene in a country, as in Turkey and South Korea. Solidarity work-such as with South Africa during the anti-apartheid movement-can be a model for other situations. Learning across borders took place between Seabrook, Wyhl, and Markolsheim and between Israel and South Africa. International participation was key to the International Antimilitarist Marches, the Bombspotting campaign, and the 15th of May activities in Turkey. The work of building alternatives to violence and against human rights violations in conflict areas was helped by key contributions from the nonviolence movements of Chile and Colombia.

When planning your campaigns, it is always good to research if others have done something similar before and to learn from their successes and errors. And remember to document your own campaigns, sharing your stories. We hope that the following stories serve as inspiration for your nonviolent strategies. War Resisters' International, which played a role in connecting people in most of these cases, supports exchange and support among nonviolent and antimilitarist movements, believing it is crucial to create an international movement against war and for peace and justice.

International Solidarity Campaign with South Africa

Howard Clark

The first calls for an international boycott of apartheid South Africa were made as early as 1958; in Britain, the Anti-Apartheid Movement launched in 1959 saw it as a major strategy. At the intergovernmental level, South Africa's system of apartheid was widely condemned, especially after the 1960 Sharpeville massacre. In 1961 South Africa was thrown out of the Commonwealth (then called the British Commonwealth), and in 1962 the UN set up a Special Committee Against Apartheid, the next year agreeing to a 'voluntary' arms embargo. Yet apartheid did not finally end until the 1990s.

There were three main areas for international sanctions against South Africa: economic sanctions, including trade and investment; a cultural boycott; and a sports boycott. The cultural and sports boycotts had primarily a psychological impact on South Africa. A sports-mad country, South Africa's exclusion from the Olympics from 1964 onwards, and most importantly from international rugby and cricket from 1970 onwards, was brought about by a combination of pressure from other African states and demonstrations, including disrupting tennis and rugby matches.

The impact of economic sanctions remains a matter of debate, especially because two powerful states (Britain and the USA) repeatedly circumvented the declarations of intergovernmental organisations such as the UN or the Commonwealth. However, there were waves of movements for 'people's sanctions' — beginning probably with the revulsion at the Sharpeville massacre — when even the British Labour Party leadership supported the moral gesture of refusing to buy South African fruit.

My own involvement began later. As a student in 1969, I was one of those who wanted to transfer the momentum gained from the sporting boycott into an economic boycott. Our students' union had already passed resolutions against the university buying apartheid fruit. Then we took up a campaign against Barclays Bank, the most popular bank for British students at that time and, as it happened, the bank used by my university. Our first success was in dissuading new students from opening their first-ever bank accounts with Barclays and persuading others to change banks. Our second was in holding a rent strike, refusing to pay rent for student rooms into an account with Barclays Bank. Eventually the university authorities conceded, triggering the resignation of prominent members of the University's ruling council. Throughout the country, trade union branches, clubs, associations, and churches debated changing banks. I got into trouble with both the Quakers and the Peace Pledge Union for writing in *Peace News* in 1972 that they had no legitimacy in talking about nonviolence in South Africa unless they took the small step of moving their bank accounts. Local authorities decided to do so too. In 1986-16 years after the Boycott Barclays campaign began — the bank sold its South African subsidiaries.

Finally, too, the Cooperative supermarket chain decided not to stock South African products.

This type of boycott was very much influenced by waves of concern about apartheid. One such wave was after the Soweto killings of 1976 and the murder in custody of Steve Biko in 1977; another was in the 1980s with the emergence inside South Africa of the United Democratic Front and spokespeople such as Desmond Tutu. All the while, in the background, were local anti-apartheid activists, putting resolutions to their trade union branches and their churches, recognising that both trade unions and churches were large corporate investors capable of exerting pressure on companies.

In Britain, the anti-apartheid boycott was a 'long march', usually rather unspectacular. Having succeeded in persuading municipal councils to do something, we then had to witness Margaret Thatcher's government take away their power to make decisions on such political grounds. Nevertheless, we kept the issue of Britain's connections with apartheid in people's minds.

The story was different in other countries. In the 1970s we Brits looked enviously at the success of the Dutch boycott of coffee from Angola, a Portuguese colony in close alliance with South Africa. In the 1980s, workers at one of Ireland's main supermarket chains — Dunne's — were locked out in a four-year dispute over selling apartheid goods, a conflict only resolved when the Irish government made South African products illegal.

The USA was a particularly important terrain of struggle. The people's sanctions' movement had three main foci: colleges and campuses; banks; and municipal and state corporations. Their achievements were considerable. In 1985, after a 19-year campaign, the main bank involved with South Africa — Chase Manhattan — announced that it would not renew its loans to South African projects. By 1991, 28 states, 24 counties, 92 cities, and the Virgin Islands had adopted legislation or policies imposing some form of sanctions on South Africa. By the end of 1987 more than 200 U.S. companies had formally withdrawn from South Africa, though many of them found other ways to carry on their business. (For instance, General Motors licensed local production, while IBM computers had a South African distributor.) What was most important about these campaigns, however, was the public education carried out through them and the sense of solidarity engendered with the anti-apartheid movement inside South Africa.

Seabrook-Wyhl-Marckolsheim: Transnational Links in a Chain of Campaigns

Joanne Sheehan and Eric Bachman

THE SEABROOK SITE, NEW HAMPSHIRE, USA, 1977.   PHOTO: GRACE HEDERMANN

When 18 people walked onto the construction site of the Seabrook Nuclear Power Plant in New Hampshire on 1 August 1976, it was the first collective nonviolent direct action against nuclear power in the USA. Many opponents of nuclear power considered such tactics too radical. Later that month, when 180 people committed civil disobedience at the site, the organisers, the Clamshell Alliance, used nonviolence training and the affinity group structure for the first time. In the future, these elements became well-known and practised throughout the nonviolent social change movement. On 30 April 1977 over 2400 people, organised in hundreds of affinity groups, occupied the site. During the next two days 1415 were arrested, many jailed for two weeks. This action inspired the anti-nuclear power movement and created a new international model for organising actions that consisted of training for nonviolent direct action and consensus decision-making in a non-hierarchical affinity group structure.

Inspiration for the Seabrook action actually came from Europe. In the early 1970s, people in Germany and France became concerned about plans to build a nuclear power plant in Whyl, Germany. Nearby, across the border in Marckolsheim, France, a German company announced plans to build a lead factory alongside the Rhine. The people living in Whyl and Marckolsheim agreed to cooperate in a cross-border campaign, in August 1974 founding a joint organisation, the International Committee of 21 Environmental Groups from Baden (Germany) and Alsace (France). Together they decided that wherever the construction started first, together they would nonviolently occupy that site to stop the plants.

After workers began constructing a fence for the Marckolsheim lead plant, on 20 September 1974 local women climbed into the fencepost holes and stopped the construction. Environmental activists erected a tent, at first outside the fence line, but soon moved inside and occupied the site. Support for the campaign came from many places. The German anarcho-pacifist magazine

Graswurzelrevolution had helped to spread the idea of grassroots nonviolent actions. A local group from Freiburg, Germany, near the plants, introduced active nonviolence to those organising in Whyl and Marckolsheim. In 1974, a 3-day workshop in Marckolsheim included nonviolence training; 300 people practised role-plays and planned what to do if the police came.

People from both sides of the Rhine — farmers, housewives, fisherfolk, teachers, environmentalists, students and others — built a round, wooden 'Friendship House' on the site. The occupation in Marckolsheim continued through the winter, until 25 February 1975 when the French government withdrew the construction permit for the lead works.

Meanwhile, construction of the nuclear reactor in Whyl, Germany, had begun. The first occupation of that site began on 18 February 1975 but was stopped by the police a few days later. After a transnational rally of 30,000 people on 23 February, the second occupation of the Whyl construction site began. Encouraged by the success in Marckolsheim, the environmental activists, including whole families from the region, continued this occupation for eight months. More than 20 years of legal battles finally ended the plans for the construction of the Whyl nuclear power plant.

In the summer of 1975, two U.S. activists, Randy Kehler and Betsy Corner, visited Whyl after attending the War Resisters' International Triennial in the Netherlands. They brought the film *Lovejoy's Nuclear War*, the story of the first individual act of nonviolent civil disobedience against a nuclear power plant in the United States. They brought back to the United States and to those organising to stop the Seabrook nuclear power plant the inspiring story of the German community's occupations. More information exchange followed. During the 1976 occupation of Seabrook, WRI folks in Germany communicated daily by phone with the Clamshell Alliance. German nonviolent activists had been using consensus, but the affinity group structure was new to them, and they saw it as a excellent method for organising actions.

In 1977, German activists and trainers Eric Bachman and Günter Saathoff made a speaking trip to the United States, visiting anti-nuclear groups in the northeastern United States as well as groups in California where there were protests against a nuclear power plant at Diablo Canyon. Activists from both sides of the Atlantic continued this process of cross-fertilisation.

The Marckolsheim and Whyl plants were never built. Even though one of the two proposed nuclear reactors was built in Seabrook, no new nuclear power plants have started in the United States since then. Both Whyl in Germany and Seabrook in the United States were important milestones for the anti-nuclear movement and encouraged many other such campaigns.

The Clamshell Alliance at Seabrook, which was itself inspired by actions in Europe, in turn became a source of inspiration to others in the USA and in Europe. In the United States, the Seabrook action inspired the successful campaign to stop the Shoreham, Long Island, New York, nuclear power plant, then 80 percent completed. That began when an affinity group of War Resisters League members returned from the Seabrook occupation and began to organise in their community. British activists who took part in the 1977 occupation of

Seabrook, together with activists who read about it in *Peace News*, decided to promote this form of organisation in Britain, leading to the Torness Alliance opposing the last 'green field' nuclear site in Britain. In Germany, a number of nuclear power plants and nuclear fuel reprocessing plants were prevented or closed due to growing protests. In the early 1980s, large nonviolent actions were organised in both Britain and Germany in opposition to the installation of U.S. cruise missiles, using the affinity group model. And the story has continued, with affinity groups being used in many nonviolent actions around the world (including in the 1999 sit-ins in Seattle to stop the World Trade Organisation meetings).

International Antimilitarist Marches

Milan

The International Nonviolent March for Demilitarisation (IMD) was an annual event in Europe from 1976 until 1989 that helped spread the idea of organising through affinity groups and using nonviolence training and consensus decision-making.

I attended four of the marches and was involved in organising three: 1983 in Brussels against the IDEE (electronic defence exhibition), 1984 Grebenhain (Fulda-Gap, blocking military maneuvers), and 1985 in Denmark (against Nuclear Arms).

My first blockade was in 1979 at Ramstein. We were organised in affinity groups, making decisions by consensus and with a speakers' council (one 'speaker' from each affinity group). Nearly all camps, marches, and bigger actions after that were organised in that way. It looked as if this idea of non-hierarchical ways of organising nonviolent direct action was spreading, but it might be simply that those were the kind of events I chose to attend.

In 1982 I attended my first 'Training for Trainers' where we learnt more about the affinity group system and consensus decision-making. During the 1980s, there was a big demand for nonviolent trainings and one of the regular topics was 'non-hierarchical ways of organising nonviolent direct action'.

I found the intercultural profile of the IMD very empowering and think that many participants were enthused to go home to spread the ideas and forms of organising. Also, we could use the attraction of an international event to draw in more and different people than would have happened with a purely locally organised event.

On these marches we also connected related themes. For instance, I learnt about gestalt therapy as a way of confronting personal patterns that restrict our creativity. This is happening with the G8 actions/camps today. One reporter commented that 'perhaps the biggest political impact of these days will happen when these young men and women go home, back to their 'normal' life — changed by this experience, empowered and nurtured by the actions they did, and by the support they have given and received'.

98

A good experience is like a seed that rests for a while in fertile ground and then grows, becoming perhaps a pretty fly or a nourishing vegetable. For me — and I think for many others — the IMD planted such seeds.

Chile: Gandhi's Insights Gave People Courage to Defy Chile's Dictatorship

Roberta Bacic

On 11 September 1973, the Chilean junta, backed by the United States's CIA and Nixon Administration, overthrew the democratically elected government of socialist president Salvador Allende. Priscilla Hayner, in her book *Unspeakable Truths, Confronting State Terror and Atrocity* (2001), outlines the devastating impact of the resulting dictatorship: 'The regime espoused a virulent anticommunism to justify its repressive tactics, which included mass arrests, torture (estimates of the number of people tortured range from 50,000 to 200,000), killings, and disappearances'. The dictatorship assassinated, tortured, and exiled thousands of political opponents and visionaries.

Under these conditions, a foreboding silence, the result of threats and terror, hung over Chile. Some of us wondered if Gandhian insights about the power of nonviolence could help in the struggle to defy the terror.

(Nonviolence refers to a philosophy and strategy of conflict resolution, a means of fighting injustice, and — in a broader sense — a way of life, developed and employed by Gandhi and by followers around the world. Nonviolence is action that does not do or allow injustice.)

Crying Out the Truth

A few of us decided to try to inspire others to speak up against the dictatorship by 'crying out the truth'. We faced a double suffering: the pain involved in enduring the dictatorship's violence and the suffering caused by keeping silent out of fear. To not cry out while those we love were killed, tortured, and disappeared was unendurable. Clandestine pamphlets and leaflets were printed. Slogans that denounced human rights violations were painted on the walls at night, at great risk to safety. Underlying these actions was the principle of active nonviolence: since injustice exists, we are first required to report it, otherwise we are accomplices. The clandestine actions helped spread the principle of telling the truth and acting on it. Yet, despite the risks, we needed to move beyond clandestine protests: we needed to move the protests against the Chilean junta into the public arena.

Activating the Public Movement against Torture

José Aldunate, a Jesuit priest who became the leader of the Sebastian Acevedo Movement Against Torture in Chile, says in his memoirs, 'A comrade came to us and brought up the fact (of torture). We educated ourselves about torture and

DEMONSTRATION OF THE SEBASTIAN ACEVEDO MOVEMENT, SANTIAGO, CHILE.
PHOTO: ARCHIVES OF ROBERTA BACIC

about the dynamics of nonviolence. We watched a film on Mahatma Gandhi. I was more motivated [to protest against] poverty, but I responded to the discipline of the group. We deliberated and decided to undertake a nonviolent demonstration to denounce torture . . . to break the barriers of silence and hiding with regards to torture, we had an obligation to denounce it in public. We needed to shake the population's conscience'.

On 14 September 1983, ten years after the regime took power, the anti-torture movement was born in an action in front of the headquarters of the National Investigation Centre in Santiago. Around 70 people interrupted traffic, unfurling a banner that read 'Torturing Done Here'. They shouted their denunciation and sang a hymn to liberty. The group returned to this scene to denounce the regime's crimes against humanity at least once a month until 1990. The movement denounced torture. It left to other entities the task of investigating and making declarations.

In order to act, we needed to openly defy the State of Emergency provisions that the junta had decreed in order to terrorise the population. We needed to break through our own sense of powerlessness, isolation, and fear. But we also needed to provide some measures of safety. The movement had no meeting place, no secretariat, no infrastructure. It met in the streets and plazas when it was time to act. It had no membership list. Participants came by personal invitation, as the movement had to avoid infiltration from the secret police and other repressive institutions. Instructions were passed from person to person. Participants were mainly trained during the actions themselves, where we evaluated each action on the spot.

Participants faced legal and illegal sanctions when detained and prosecuted, as they often were. Tear gas, beatings, detention, and prosecution were common retaliatory practices used against demonstrators. Torture was also a possible consequence of being arrested. Not only the Sebastian Acevedo movement participants face these sanctions; so did reporters and journalists willing to report on the actions and the issues that were exposed. Some of the actions had as many as 300 participants. Some 500 people participated in total. There were Christians and non-Christians, priests, monks, slum dwellers, students, aged people, homemakers, and members of various human rights movements — people of every class, ideology, and walk of life.

The main goal was to end torture in Chile. The means chosen was to shake up national awareness (consciousness raising) and rouse the conscience of the nation until the regime got rid of torture or the country got rid of the regime. In 1988, after a widespread anti-intimidation campaign, the nonviolent 'Chile Sí, Pinochet No' campaign helped, to Pinochet's shock, to defeat a plebiscite designed to ratify Pinochet's rule.

Efforts to end the culture of impunity that arose during the Pinochet years and to engage in national reconciliation continue, but nonviolent protest provided an important means, amongst others, to overthrow the dictatorship.

Israel: New Profile Learns from the Experience of Others

Ruth Hiller

There was a new political awareness in Israel in the mid-nineties. Increasing numbers of people objected to Israeli's presence in Lebanon and the loss of Israeli lives. Some questioned the government's incursion into Palestinian lands. Demonstrations took place daily, particularly at major road junctions, to pressure Israel to get out of Lebanon. Several groups led the grassroots movements at the time: Four Mothers, Mothers and Women for Peace, and Women in Black.

My son had decided to refuse military conscription, and I needed to get more involved. I started to look for people who were examining things critically, hoping to find a support group. I had a neighbour who was a social activist; we started going to demonstrations at the junction close to home. There I heard a woman address the crowd about getting even more involved. I called her the next day. She told me about a study group that had just started meeting on a monthly basis. The group was comprised of middle and upper middle class white (of European descent as opposed to Mizrachi, Ethiopian, or Palestinian Israeli) women, most like myself, looking for some way to consider change together. Some were already active in the peace movement; some had lost family members in war.

In the study group I learned to look at things with a critical, feminist eye.

ACTION IN FRONT OF THE ISRAELI MINISTRY OF DEFENCE, TEL AVIV, ISRAEL.   PHOTO: ANDREAS SPECK

Rela Mazali, a feminist, author, and activist in the peace and human rights movements for many years, facilitated. She brought materials that we analysed to understand why things are the way they are. Why is Israel a militarist power? Why is there so much discrimination in Israel? What are the similarities between the pyramid of power in the military and civilian life in Israel? What is victimisation? What are the roles of women and mothers? What is Jewish heritage, and what role does it play in Israel today? (And many more relative issues.)

We talked about effective movements from which we could learn. We looked at two different but related South African groups that worked to end apartheid. They are important examples of the power of small focus groups who work in a spiral motion and gain momentum.

We studied South Africa's End Conscription Campaign, launched by various CO groups in 1983 to oppose conscription in the service of apartheid. In 1985, after white troops were deployed in black townships, the number of conscripts who did not respond to the call-ups increased by 500 percent' (from a short history at http://www.wri-irg.org/co/rtba/southafrica.htm). We discussed the End Conscription Campaign through Rela's study and research in her ongoing reading about militarisation — first through Jacklyn Cock's book, *Women & War in South Africa*. We then continued with an email exchange with her and others.

We also studied the Black Sash Movement, a group of nonviolent white women who used the safety of their privilege to challenge the apartheid system. They displayed black sashes to express their disgust at the racist system. They tied them to trees, posts, on car antennas, anywhere they could be seen by all. We tried to use an orange sash similar to the black sash used in South Africa, tying them everywhere possible. But it never took off; it didn't work at the time. (The Black Sash Movement had been an inspiration for Women in Black, which was founded in Israel in 1987.)

But we did find another aspect of their work very helpful. While we had read about this, we also learned from some South African women, one white, one black, and one of Indian descent, who, in 1999, facilitated a seminar bringing together Israeli women in the Left. South Africans couldn't congregate in groups of more than three. So they met in groups of three, then one of them would meet with two more people. The South Africans worked in that circular movement, using this deeper way of networking to spread their message and engage in dialogue about ending conscription. We learned important lessons: it's a matter of discussing with people, not lecturing. Even if you find someone who agrees with you on only one thing, build on that one thing. One on one, or one with a very small group, is more effective. It takes a lot of energy to organise. Everyday life is hard; it takes a lot to be an activist. But putting the time into this kind of process can be deep and effective.

'For our first open study day in October 1998,' Rela recalls, 'I wrote up the main principles formulated and followed by the End Conscription Campaign and gave a short talk also proposing possible similarities and differences as I saw them. We returned to these questions from time to time at various points in our meetings, discussions, organising, etc.' In retrospect, we realise this was our founding conference. We were not looking to form a movement. We really wanted to gather together and learn. The events of the day and the fact that over 150 people showed up to discuss and learn made it clear that there were people we could work with.

My son being a pacifist may have been a major factor in our group discussions of the issue of conscription and the right to conscience. Some felt that conscientious objection was too radical and later left the group. But about 12 of the original 30 or so women who had been members of what had grown into two study groups are still active in New Profile today. In August 2000, New Profile discussed initiating an End Conscription Campaign. However, the Intifada started a month later, sidetracking that idea. We are just getting back to that now with our new campaign 'Thinking Before Enlistment'. New Profile recognises conscription as one part of the militarisation of Israel. Even if the Occupation ended, we still have to demilitarise Israeli society.

New Profile has maintained a learning/action balance. We have internal study days as well as open sessions. We have learning circles five to seven times a year. Sometimes we focus on a very specific issue during our monthly plenary. This is usually without guest speakers and focuses on different aspects of what can become a basis for action. But for separate study days and learning circles we may have guest speakers. But sometimes the facilitator is someone from within the group who has learned about something in particular or is an expert in the matter. We want to discover more and learn about it collectively; New Profile is non-hierarchical. We have remained an active organisation, working without a managerial board for 10 years. Nothing is ever done single-handedly or without analysis. Nothing changes overnight: to really make change happen, we need to be persistent. Our studying of effective movements made that clear.

＊ *See also 'An Example of Linking Peace and Gender Issues', p26.*

Turkey: Building a Nonviolent Culture

Hilal Demir and Ferda Ülker

Militarism and patriarchy are deeply rooted in Turkish culture. Currently, war in the 'south-east' is based on ethnic discrimination against Kurds, although it is officially described as a 'war against terrorism'. Any attempt to question militarism is called 'treason'. The people most affected by the negative consequences of violence are primarily women, children, and elders and also religious, ethnic, and political minorities. Violence is so internalised in Turkish society that alternative perspectives have been made unthinkable, even among those who normally question hierarchy and promote freedom and equality.

The influence of the military can be seen in the following examples:

■ Only after having done military service is a man regarded as a 'real' man.
■ The National Security Council (including the chiefs of staff) as recently as 1997 prevented the winners of the elections from forming a government ("the post-modern coup').
■ Economic power: the Turkish army's financial services company OYAK is one of the most powerful investors in Turkey.
■ Opinion polls show that the military is the institution most trusted by the people.

The army under Mustafa Kemal established the Turkish republic in 1923, after the collapse of the Ottoman Empire; Kemalist principles remain fundamental to the state, reflected in the criminal code, the maintenance of a powerful army, and the belief in the 'indivisibility of the nation'. These generate repressive attitudes. Few people see male domination of women as an issue, and physical violence is widely accepted against subordinates, prisoners, and within the family.

Beginnings

The term nonviolence was used for the first time in the principles of the Izmir War Resisters' Association (IWRA) in 1992. Within the Association, nonviolence was always a discussion point, especially how to find practical ways of living nonviolently in a violent culture. We first used nonviolence training to prepare ourselves for prison visit scenarios when a group member, Osman Murat Ülke, was imprisoned for conscientious objection. Initially nobody from outside approached us to discuss nonviolence. However, now there is more interest, although the War Resisters' Association itself closed in 2001 because of the burn-out of members.

IWRA's commitment to nonviolence put us in sharp contrast with other leftist groups who did not take our approach seriously and regarded nonviolence as weak and ineffective. We mainly involved antimilitarist, anarchist, and feminist activists. Perhaps the biggest welcome for nonviolence came from the Lesbian, Gay, Bi,- and Trans-sexual (LGBT) movement which was just in the process of becoming structured and took up nonviolent methods.

In political alliances, our most fruitful interaction was with the women's movement. When we first began, we formed a feminist and antimilitarist women's group called 'Antimilitarist Feminists', trying to reach out to women's groups. Despite some initial disappointment, we reached many independent women and began to hold trainings with women's organisations. This change in attitude was related to changes/transformation within the women's movement, in particular a desire to do things their own way rather than on traditional leftist lines. Questioning violence became a priority for women, and nonviolence seemed to offer a response. As more women sought personal empowerment, our cooperation with women and women's groups strengthened.

The closest political group was the conscientious objection movement because it was built by the efforts of activists working to promote nonviolence. Although this partnership continues, an individualistic streak in the movement, we believe, makes discussion of nonviolence less effective. Although most Turkish conscientious objectors are total resisters (that is, rejecting both military service and any civilian substitute), the movement's attitude towards nonviolence is equivocal at times, especially because of support for conscientious objectors from the Kurdish movement and leftist groups.

Izmir Nonviolent Trainers Initiative

The Izmir Nonviolent Trainers Initiative (INTI) was first formed as part of the IWRA with additional support from others. Our work was supported and improved in quality thanks to cooperation with German trainers, including training courses at Kurve Wustrow in Germany, an international training for trainers organised in Foca, Turkey, in April 1996, and the accompaniment of two German trainers who lived in Izmir from 1998 until 2001.

When IWRA closed in December 2001, the trainers' initiative continued, organising workshops in Izmir and anywhere in the country we are invited, including in Diyarbakir in the south-east 'crisis' region. Today five trainers — four female and one male — mostly work on a voluntary basis, only receiving travel expenses, although sometimes we have money to pay a part-time coordinator. In June 2006 we began a course of training for trainers with 20 participants from all over the country.

The aim of INTI is to enhance and establish nonviolent principles and structures as an alternative to militarism, nationalism, hierarchy, and patriarchy.

Our public activities began with organising demonstrations and seminars on nonviolence and conscientious objection, publishing pamphlets (although police confiscated a number of our works from printers), and looking for international cooperation. In the field of training we worked with activists from extra-parliamentary groups, from human rights, women's, and LGBT groups, and from political parties. Additionally, the group co-operated with the Human Rights Centre of the Izmir Lawyers' Association to train lawyers and police about human rights issues. In general, issues covered in our trainings include creating non-hierarchical structures for grassroots and oppositional political work, consensus decision-making, discussion of militaristic structures within society (starting from the family), and nonviolent alternatives. The individual behaviours and actions of participants are always the basic and central point of our workshops. We reflect on theoretical analyses and practical experiences of nonviolence and nonviolent actions (starting with Henry David Thoreau and Mohandas Gandhi and leading to today's examples). We include reflections on anarchistic approaches to nonviolence, on Augusto Boal's Theatre of the Oppressed, and Gene Sharp's strategies of nonviolence.

Our group believes that it is possible to eliminate all kinds of inequalities, discrimination, and thus violence and to develop nonviolent actions and methods for social and political change. Therefore, with the principle that 'nonviolence is not an aspiration to be achieved in the future, but the very means to achieve such a goal', our group started questioning everyday life practices that may seem to be 'neutral'. For over ten years our group has been learning, practising, and teaching the means and methods of nonviolence, an attitude towards life that we are now developing as a life principle.

First, we offer 'introductory' one-day trainings for diverse organisations and for individual activists who question violence within their agendas. Second, we offer 'issue-based trainings' on particular topics requested by groups based on their needs; these have included prejudice, conflict resolution, communication, and sexism. Third, we are working to offer a one-week intensive 'training for trainers' session with individuals who have taken part in the first two training sessions and who want to become trainers; this was in response to a constantly increasing demand for such a module. Since 2002, we have conducted the first and second parts of trainings with diverse groups — working with women, the LGBT community, and human rights, ecology, peace, and antimilitarist groups in Izmir, Ankara, Antalya, Adana, and Diyarbakir.

Individuals who participated in our first two trainings and wanted to be trainers had already started questioning violence and had been trying to integrate nonviolent methods in their institutions and their individual practices. However, they felt they lacked information and experience about 'nonviolent action'. For example, in Diyarbakir we identified a need to learn about developing nonviolent solutions for fundamental activities (like 'honour' killings, violence against women, etc). Participants needed empowerment for their work and an enhanced capacity to use nonviolence to create new solutions to ongoing problems.

TRAINING FOR TRAINERS IN TURKEY. PHOTO: HILAL DEMIR

We are aware that it is impossible to cover all principles of nonviolence in a one-week training. One of the solutions we found is to continue dialogue and to seek possibilities for future meetings of supervision and feedback. Furthermore, during our third training, we plan to form a network between trainers from all over Turkey and will establish operational principles for such a network. This 'network of trainers' approach will ensure that our dialogue is sustainable and allow us to continue sharing knowledge and experience among nonviolence trainers and to collaboratively disseminate nonviolence training both at local and national levels.

Our Aims

We aim to improve and strengthen the culture of democracy and human rights by introducing the concept of nonviolence, to question the culture of violence (which has a militaristic and patriarchal character in Turkey) in order to sow seeds of a culture of nonviolence, and to raise awareness of and struggle with discrimination in all walks of life. Training trainers will allow them to work for these ends by gaining practical experience and increasing their capacity to facilitate their own training groups.

Nonviolent Campaigns

Looking at examples of nonviolent campaigns in Turkey, we can say that these activities have not been organised in an entirely nonviolent way. While nonviolence was one of the fundamental principles, some organisations lacked some

107

of the qualities of a truly nonviolent action, such as preparing for the event with nonviolence trainings. One of the longest campaigns in this regard was the Militourism Festival. This festival, held annually on 15th of May (International Conscientious Objectors' Day), consisted of visiting prominent militarist symbols in various cities, organising alternative events, and declarations of conscientious objections. Another was the 'We Are Facing It' Campaign, aimed at coming to terms with the war going on in Turkey. It was spread over an entire year, with major actions held every three months. The aim was to prevent people from ignoring this war by the use of nonviolent means such as street theatre. Another nonviolent action was the 'Rice Day', held in Ankara, the centre of official administration, and specifically in front of a military barracks. We gathered there to say 'we exist, we are here'. As antimilitarists who subverted societal roles in our activities, we used the symbol of Rice Day to enhance group solidarity and end our invisibility. Apart from these major activities, smaller organisations and actions mobilised for short-term political intervention purposes.

Epilogue

Although we have often been marginalised throughout the short history of nonviolence in Turkey and have not been as effective as we would like, we are becoming more visible thanks to alliances forged with the women's and LGBT movements. This is further aided by the fact that discussion about conscientious objection has begun in the public arena. Increasing demands from different political groups for implementing nonviolence training and methods in their programmes affirm this trend.

The Applications of Augusto Boal's 'Theatre of Oppressed'

Two books by Augusto Boal have been translated into Turkish, and various periodicals have discussed his work and 'Theatre of the Oppressed'. We generally use his methods in nonviolence trainings, especially 'sculpture theatre' and 'simultaneous dramaturgy'; we also use them in our personal lives. Boal's techniques offer simple and creative responses to stereotyped situations; for instance, if someone stares at you like a sex object, how about simply picking your nose?

Sculpture Theatre (or Image Theatre)

This method uses body language to explore concepts. Participants are asked to 'sculpt' their (or others') bodies to express an idea. Then they move into a group to form a group 'sculpture' or image. We have explored concepts such as 'war' and 'peace'; for instance, using the form of the participants' bodies and their relation to each other to express different aspects of conflict in the dynamics of war. We also ask the group to 'dynamise' the group sculpture of war, transforming into peace. This stimulates an enjoyable and active atmosphere in which to discuss the obstacles we face during the transition from 'war' to 'peace'.

Forum theatre (or 'simultaneous dramaturgy')

One method is to act out a scenario in which something happens that you want to prevent or change. Then you re-enact the scenario; members of the audience can interrupt, calling out 'freeze' and making a suggestion for something that one of the characters might do differently. The person who calls out then takes over the role of that character and tests out the idea. We have used this with groups of up to 20 women using the scenario of sexual harassment at a bus stop or during bus trips. Participants are asked: 'what can she do to prevent the harassment'? When a person offers a suggestion, they enter the scenario to test out the idea. We personally practise a course of action that we learned from this study and share this experience with other groups and people. (See 'Forum Theatre' Exercise, p137.)

Invisible theatre

This is a performance either in the streets or somewhere unexpected, rather than a theatre. A good place to do this in Izmir is on the ferry, especially at rush hour. One year on 25 November — the international day against violence against women — we dramatised a scene of a man harassing a women. Others of our group mingled with passengers and started a discussion, explaining at the end of the short ferry trip that the male harasser was playing a role and was really a friend, but that women confront this situation daily. After our second experience of invisible theatre, we invited passengers to a press conference afterwards. Some women who attended wanted to keep in touch. Once we did 'invisible theatre' about children and violence, but when we finished, a participant protested that we had exposed him to a disturbing dramatisation against his will.

Newspaper Theatre

This method is generally used during street actions, especially when making press statements or petitioning against human rights violations. It creates an opportunity to attract people's attention. We created our own newspaper that looked like an ordinary Turkish newspaper and read it on a stage to the public. We used this technique to show and get the attention of the public about a fact of our daily lives: that there is still war and that while the media do not cover it, we need to be aware of it.

✱ *For more on the Theatre of the Oppressed, visit
http://www.theatreoftheoppressed.org.*

Challenges and Successes of Working with Nonviolence in South Korea

Jungmin Choi

N ot long ago, Korean social movements began to use the concept of 'non-violent way of struggle'. Still, many social activists see nonviolence negatively, as a weak, passive, non-resistant form of struggle, partly because of our own history.

For more than 30 years after the Japanese colonial occupation and then the Korean War, an authoritarian military regime ruled South Korea. The regime responded to growing aspirations for liberty and democracy with armed terror, and so some people armed themselves, speaking of 'resistant violence'. Nowadays, the state still uses violence, especially against activists, but more activists are coming to accept that there is a nonviolent way of struggle.

There has been some form of nonviolent resistance since the 1980s, such as students objecting to being sent to the northern frontier, soldiers denouncing the violence they experienced during military service, and civilians protesting questioning by police patrols. However, the concept of nonviolence was limited to a means of resistance.

Now, conscientious objectors to compulsory military service are said to be the first sincere pacifists in Korea who view nonviolence as a philosophy of life. They have advocated the right to refuse unreasonable orders from the state

ANTI FLAG SWEARING DIREC ACTION, SEOUL, SOUTH KOREA.   PHOTO: JUNGMIN CHOI

(when nationalism and militarism are prevalent), and they have appealed to the basic good in people, asking them to fundamentally question the military, arms, and war. People were deeply moved when they saw conscientious objectors willing to go to prison for 18 months rather than take up arms. They have come to know the significance of the act of conscientious objection, watching the continual wars caused by the USA and Israel.

The working group for conscientious objection in Korea is now focusing on providing necessary assistance such as legal and psychological counselling to those who prepare to object and is also spreading awareness about conscientious objection through a variety of activities, such as press conferences, forums, campaigns, and direct actions. The number of conscientious objectors (COs) in Korea is still small, and the demands on those who make a conscientious objection declaration mean that they need support.

The CO movement does not have a clear stance towards nonviolent action. For instance, in 2003 when Kang Chul-min declared his conscientious objection, while he was doing his military service, there were conflicting opinions on whether to hold a sit-down demonstration in solidarity. Similar discussions arose concerning university students who made CO declarations before they were called up. Many do not see conscientious objection as one form of nonviolent direct action that should connect with other forms of direct action.

Other groups that take nonviolent pacifism as a principled philosophy played an important part in the struggle against the U.S. Military base extension in Pyeongtaek. They used diverse tactics, including imaginative forms of nonviolent direct action that were in striking contrast to previous methods of struggle. Some campaigners decided to make a 'peace village', squatting in buildings abandoned to make way for the base and renovating them as a library, café and guesthouse, displaying works of art donated by artists. When bulldozers, backed with armed riot police and private security forces ('hired thugs'), arrived to demolish the remaining buildings in the village, villagers and supporters initially succeeded in blocking the demolition, climbing on to roofs or tying themselves to buildings and sitting down in front of bulldozers. However as government forces escalated — from a force of 4,000 in March 2006 to 22,000 in September — hundreds of villagers and supporters were arrested or injured. Despite this, people still tried to farm the fields under military occupation, finally giving up in February 2007. The last candlelight vigil of protest was held in March 2007; the next month villagers and supporters returned to bury a time capsule marked by a flag saying 'Return'.

Peace Community of San José de Apartadó, Colombia: A Lesson of Resistance, Dignity, and Courage

Ruben Dario Pardo Santamaria

Founded in 1997, the Peace Community of San José de Apartadó was born in adverse conditions for nonviolent resistance. The Community is located in an area of Uraba, Colombia, where strong economic interests are at play and where armed conflict is waged between guerrillas (the FARC), state forces, and paramilitaries (usually working in collusion with the state). It is an area where political terror, assassination, and intimidation have been used to eliminate leaders and activists. The Peace Community itself is formed of displaced people, people whose parents and grandparents were also victims of violence. Throughout its existence, the Peace Community has faced campaigns to discredit it from the highest levels of national government and the media, especially under the government of Alvaro Uribe.

The Peace Community has more than 1,000 members, even though around 150 members have been killed by state security forces, paramilitaries, or the FARC.

Towards a Strategy of Civil Resistance

What began with an urgent need to find practical alternatives for displaced people has grown into a project offering an alternative to the current model of society. This has three dimensions:

- Resisting war and forced displacement, establishing a mechanism for protecting civilians in a context of strong armed conflict.
- Establishing a sustainable basis for community cohesion, including developing holistic and ecological economic alternatives.
- Constructing peace at the everyday, personal level of nonviolent relationships and at political levels through condemning the use of violence and supporting a negotiated political solution to the armed conflict and through outreach, spreading the idea of zones of peace and offering guidance to other local communities.

Economic Strategy

A war zone does not have a normal supply of essential goods. Therefore, the Community needs to grow its own food; it cooperates with 'fair trade' groups to market coca and baby bananas. In addition, it organised meetings and courses (under the title Peasant University or University of Resistance) to share information about ecological forms of agriculture.

Policy Strategy

The emergence of the Peace Community has been a radical challenge to those who seek to dominate a territory, above all the armed actors of the state, the paramilitaries, and the guerrillas. To survive, the Community needs to build relationships that on the one hand reduce the pressure on the Peace Community and on the other strengthen its resilience through building relationships at the local, national, and international levels.

Community Cohesion

The Peace Community's founding declaration lays out principles of demilitarisation and neutrality that represent the common denominator of the community. The act of signing this declaration is a unifying force for the collective.

Training has been vital to the community. First, in preparing to establish the community, there were workshops with displaced people and prospective members. Now the Training Committee concentrates internally on strengthening the understanding of and commitment to the Community's principles, analysing its situation, and evaluating the whole process of civil resistance. It teaches conflict resolution skills within the Community itself and aims to strengthen the resolve of Community members not to join any armed group. The Training Committee works not only with families, coordinators, and working groups of the Community but also with other families in the area.

Protection

The Community engages in activities to reduce the risk of human rights' violations of Community members and to strengthen the very process of civil resistance. This involves:

- documenting and publicly denouncing violations committed by all armed actors;
- identifying community spaces by erecting billboards declaring its principles;
- disseminating information through small publications, videos, national and international meetings on its territory, national and international tours, and its own Website;
- petitioning the national government and increasingly international agencies, which has sometimes led to favourable verdicts such as restrictions on U.S. military aid and the trial of soldiers accused of killing Community leaders in February 2005;
- protective accompanying: Peace Brigades International regularly accompanies transport to and from the Community, while other international groups, including the U.S. Fellowship of Reconciliation, support placements in the Community, for instance, working in the school.

Proposal for New Neutral Zones

Unlike 'safe areas' created by agreement between armed forces, in the Peace Community the civilian population itself has decided to create a physical space and social protection for those not involved in the war. Peace communities are not a mere space of survival amid the bullets, but places that seek to build peace with social justice, a way of life based on dignity, autonomy, and solidarity.

Ability to Resist Repression

The peace community of San José de Apartadó has been one of the worst hit by political violence in Colombia. Political repression is aimed at breaking the principles and beliefs of those who opt for peace, at spreading mistrust and intimidation, and at crippling individual and collective action. Through selective actions and direct violence, this repression spreads intimidation and mistrust among the population, crippling peoples' capacities to react.

Persistence in the Community's resistance, despite the violence, can be partly explained by the absence of better alternatives for people who have been forcibly displaced. However, it also depends on more positive factors: a strong social consciousness, in which people act as subjects not subordinate to political orders; the perception that, despite the armed actors, the process of resistance has a chance of success; confidence that nonviolence offers better chances of survival; and an unshakable commitment not to abandon the struggle for which so many martyrs have already given their lives.

Different Types of Resistance

The Peace Community resists at many levels:

- resisting malaria, poverty, and the lack of basic services in such areas of Colombia;
- resisting the terror of legal and illegal armed groups;
- resisting the temptation to revenge in a territory where it would be extremely easy to join any armed actor and seek vengeance against an enemy;
- resisting the imposition of an exclusive and authoritarian model of society, while proposing a project of life based on a comprehensive vision of dignity and development.

Conclusion

Among the most important factors that have enabled peasants and farmers of San José de Apartadó to maintain nonviolent resistance during the past ten years are the following:

- the accompaniment of entities of the Catholic Church;
- the Community's democratic and flexible organisational structure, which strengthens the sense of belonging and community cohesion;
- improvements in the lives of women and children as compared to previous times;
- strong internal discipline, respect for the rules of conduct agreed upon, and loyalty to fundamental principles of neutrality and nonviolence;
- implementing internal measures of protection;

SAN JOSÉ DE APARTADÓ, COLOMBIA, COFFINS PROCESSION.   PHOTO: PEACE COMMUNITY

- opening up spaces for consulting with governmental actors;
- implementing economic strategies to meet basic needs in the Community;
- a progressive process of integrating and coordinating actions with other local experiences of civil resistance in different regions of Colombia;
- training new leaders;
- the example of martyrs motivating continued resistance;
- protection offered by international accompaniment;
- gradual consolidation of a network of international support in many countries;
- the moral strength of the Community and its resilience in the face of violence by armed groups.

Strategies

115

Bombspotting: Towards a European Campaign

Roel Stynen

On 8 July 1996, the International Court of Justice declared 'that the threat or use of nuclear weapons would generally be contrary to the rules of international law'. This offered peace movements an additional argument and a legal basis for actions of civil disobedience and direct actions against nuclear weapons. In Belgium, small actions of civil disobedience at NATO's headquarters and Kleine Brogel Air Force Base started a campaign, Bombspotting, that raised the issue of nuclear weapons and the legal duty to disarm.

Bombspotting was the first time many participants took part in direct action. From the outset, organisers made a big effort to enable people to take an active role in direct action without necessarily being involved for a long time in the preparation. While we encourage people to contact a regional group and we organise and actively promote nonviolent direct action trainings, we keep participation open to 'the average citizen', not only to 'the professional activist'. This means that at Bombspotting actions, a large structure, involving hundreds of volunteers, enables people to participate easily and without heavy engagement.

One important way in which we lowered the threshold for people to participate was setting up local groups. These groups, consisting of people from very

BOMBSPOTTING ACTION AT THE MINISTRY OF DEFENCE IN BRUSSELS, BELGIUM, ONJULY 8, 2006, TO COMMEMORATE THE 10TH ANNIVERSARY OF THE ICJ'S ADVISORY OPINION ON NUCLEAR WEAPONS.
PHOTO: CAROLINE DOSSCHE

different walks of life, brought the theme of nuclear weapons and the call for direct action for nuclear disarmament out of campaign meetings and onto the streets. Local mobilising efforts were much more effective than the office's national promotion campaign. Through working with local groups, we ensured that potentially interested people nearly everywhere could have face-to-face contact with people working on the campaign on the grassroots level.

For several years, we invited international activists to participate, but then we faced new challenges. How could we help create pressure on governments of NATO member states? This is still under discussion. We are far from a truly international campaign, but have had efforts and discussions that others might learn from. When you invite internationals to join in, it's easy to overlook basic things — such as food, accommodation, meeting places, transport — that can add to stress. We need to make sure the international participants have all the information they need to make decisions. We must take language problems in account, such as ensuring that people answering a home base telephone number or legal assistance can speak different languages. The internationals need time to accustom themselves and to prepare for the action, both at home and shortly before the action. In preparation, we run through the different phases of their stay and role in the action from their perspective. What information does a person need? What could help him/her feel secure and comfortable? We also consider meeting some of the international guests before, to prepare this together.

An excellent example of an instrument designed for this purpose is the *Faslane 365 Resource Pack* (http://www.faslane365.org). This booklet gives basic information on the purpose and political context of the year-long Faslane blockade and practical advice on mobilisation, tactics, training, and more, enabling groups to autonomously prepare for participation.

In our experience, nonviolent direct action training with international participants has proved very helpful. Trainings are an opportunity to go through action scenarios extensively and to prepare to handle problems and difficulties that might arise. One can have the feeling that participating in actions abroad does not bring your own campaign much further. Moreover, it is time-consuming and might cost a lot of money. On the other hand, by going to another country, you can enhance the visibility of your campaign internationally. It's very often an effective way of meeting people with whom you can work in the future.

One example is that the international participation of French Greenpeace activists inspired them to take action against the French development of new nuclear missiles. In September, during the first large demonstration against the M51 missile, about 30 Bombspotters took part in the first Bombspotting-style citizens' inspection at the Centre d'Essaies des Landes near Bordeaux. We gave advice and assistance in preparing for the action, and Bombspotting nonviolent direct action trainers returned a few months after the action to give a 'training for trainers'.

But action abroad can never replace action in your own country. Therefore, again, it is of the utmost importance to think about what you expect from the involvement of internationals in your campaign or from your own participation abroad.

There are ways to increase the significance of the international presence. At the Bombspotting XL action in 2005, where citizen inspectors targeted four different sites related to nuclear weapons in Belgium, activists were present from all NATO member countries hosting NATO nuclear weapons (the UK, the United States, Italy, Germany, Turkey, and the Netherlands) and from other countries (such as Finland, France, Greece, Portugal, and Spain). Our press work drew attention to this presence, and international delegations did their own press work in their respective countries. When working this way, it is not just a question of inviting internationals and letting them participate. A lot more work is necessary, including coordinating press efforts and dividing roles before, during, and after the action.

8

EXERCISES FOR WORKING IN NONVIOLENCE

This section describes exercises to help in developing your nonviolent campaigns and actions. These exercises can be used during nonviolence trainings, workshops, or group meetings. Exercises make our time together more participatory and contribute to the process of learning and building capacities among participants.

The exercises we have collected come from a variety of sources in our rich history. Many times these exercises have been adapted and changed over time. We expect that you will do the same, changing them to meet your needs. While most of the exercises in this section can be used for different purposes, we give some recommendations for where and how to use them best, as well as tips for the facilitator/trainer.

We hope you find these exercises useful in your process of building nonviolent campaigns and that they motivate you to search for and develop more exercises to continue to enrich the repertoire of the nonviolence movement.

Intellectual Property

Only a few of these exercises give 'credit' to particular trainers or training groups. We apologise in advance to anybody who feels he or she should have been credited as the author of a particular exercise. Please let us know so that we can rectify this on the Web and in future printed editions. However, most exercises used in nonviolence training have been passed from group to group and adapted according to new situations or styles.

Exercises

HASSLE LINE

Time: Minimum 15 minutes

Goal or purpose of the exercise: To give people an opportunity to solve a hassle or conflict using nonviolence. To practise what it feels like to be in both roles in a conflict. This is a good introductory exercise for many situations.

How it's done/facilitator's notes

Ask people to form two rows of an equal number of people facing one another. (You can add another row to play the role of observers.) Ask people to reach out to the person across from them to make sure they know with whom they will interact. Explain that there are only two roles in this exercise: everyone in one line has the same role and the people opposite them have another role; each person relates only to the person across from them. Explain the roles for each side and describe the conflict and who will start it. Give participants a few seconds of silence to get into their roles and then tell them to begin. Depending on the situation, it may be a brief hassle (less than a minute) or you can let it go longer, but not more than three or four minutes.

Then call 'stop' and debrief. Debriefing questions should include: what people did, how they felt, what ways they found to solve or deal with the conflict, what they noticed about body language, what they wish they had done, etc. (If you have a third row as observers, ask them what they saw.)

Replay the exercise, switching roles. So that people do not interact with the same person, move one line up by having the person at one end go to the other end of that line and everyone in that line shift one person.

Examples of roles

- Someone planning to engage in nonviolent action/someone close to them who is opposed to their participation
- Blockading a weapons or government facility/angry worker
- Protester/counter-protester or angry passer-by
- Protester committed to nonviolence guidelines/protester breaking nonviolence guidelines

BRAINSTORMING

Time: 15 minutes or longer
Goal or purpose of the exercise: A group technique designed to generate a large number of ideas in a limited amount of time.

How it's done/facilitator's notes

Give the group a question such as 'what is nonviolence'? Or 'how do we develop a fund-raising strategy'? Then ask the group to come up with as many ideas and responses as possible.

Here are five recommendations for holding a brainstorming session:

1. Focus on quantity: The greater the number of ideas generated, the more you have to pick from.
2. No criticism: Criticism, challenges, and discussion should be put 'on hold' until the brainstorming is done.
3. Unusual ideas are welcome: To get a good and long list of ideas, unusual ideas are welcomed.
4. Combine and improve ideas: Good ideas can be combined to form a single very good idea, as suggested by the slogan '1+1=3'.
5. A brainstorm usually starts slowly, picking up speed as ideas spark other ideas, and then slowing down again. This is why some call it 'popcorning'.

After all the ideas are listed (preferably written up for all to see), ask if people have any questions about or disagree with any of the ideas. Open this up for discussion. You may not need to come to consensus on a brainstorming session. Or you may want to sort out the answers for further discussion.

At a nonviolence training session, you are not trying to come up with a single definition to answer the question 'What is nonviolence'? But through the brainstorm, participants can share many answers to that question. It can be enlightening to do a 'What is violence'? brainstorm at the same time. Pay attention to key words. Check to make sure that words like 'power' and 'anger' don't appear only in the violence brainstorm.

SPEAK OUT

Time: 3 hours
Goal or purpose of the exercise:
■ To motivate members of a dominant group to process information about injustice.
■ To turn some power dynamics upside down so the dominant group can experience what it is like when others have an uninterrupted opportunity to dominate 'air time'.
■ To build more solidarity among those who have less power so they can better support each other in an organisation or a workshop.
■ To create a norm that the dominant group members can use to support each other to change rather than depending on those who have less power to 'teach them'.

How it's done/facilitator's notes

Explain to the full group that not all gender differences are between women and men, but that power dynamics are also based on sexual orientation and on how much a person fits the dominant cultural expectations of his or her gender. While this exercise will include separate discussions of men and women to air experiences and views, it welcomes sharing other gender dynamics. Explain that the women will share from their life experiences in response to a set of questions. The men will have the job of listening as deeply as they can, giving full attention to what they hear, without asking questions. Following this, gay men and any others who feel that their gender identification has led them to experience a lack of power in their society will also be asked to speak from their life experiences.

To work effectively, this process requires common ground rules.
■ Confidentiality — Nobody should repeat outside the session what someone else has said.
■ Participants will ask permission of a person if they want to pursue a point made by that Speak Out participant.

Ask the women to go to another room with a female facilitator and prepare to speak out. They will first work on their feelings about doing this, being reassured that not everyone needs to talk and that previous experiences with this exercise have built unity. Go over the following questions and ask participants to tell personal stories about their experiences as women.

- What are you pleased about or proud of regarding your gender identity?
- What is difficult and painful about it?
- What do you want the others to know, so that they could work with you better and be more supportive?

Encourage honesty and expressing the emotions that come up.

At this same time, ask the the men to stay in the room and to work with a male facilitator who first asks about their feelings. Ask what they've found useful in their lives to enable themselves to listen well to something important they may have had difficulty hearing. Try to get as many men as possible talking. Listen for and encourage gay men and others to speak up who may have a minority status because of gender issues.

When the women are ready, they return. They stand in front of the men, who are seated, and speak as individuals (not as a group). They speak to each of the three questions, as the facilitator presents them.

Any men who also feel their gender identity has given them a minority status in their culture are invited to stand up and answer the same questions.

When the women are finished, they leave the room. The female facilitator goes with them, encouraging them to debrief.

The male facilitator assists the men in processing and digesting what they've heard and what they learnt from it.

Staying in touch, the facilitators arrange a common time to bring the two groups together.

A good tool to use is a closing circle, in which everyone gets to share one insight — usually something they've learned about themselves — in a sentence or two. The facilitators might bridge the gap by socialising with participants from the other gender group. Then play by moving into dancing or some physical activity in which everyone can participate and relax.

* This has been adapted from an exercise developed by Training for Change, notes by George Lakey, which can be found at http://trainingforchange.org/content/view/282/39/

A GENDER DIALOGUE FOR PEACEBUILDERS

Time: 30 to 45 minutes
Goal or purpose of the exercise:
- To create a space for dialogue between women and men in peace organisations.
- To identify points of tensions between men and women in peace organisations.
- To develop a level of comfort and commitment in addressing gender issues in peace organisations.

How it's done/facilitator's notes

I. Small group discussion of Gender, Conflict, and Peacebuilding
1. In mixed small groups of men and women, make a list of the ways men and women experience conflict and violence differently.
2. In the same small groups, make a list of the different ways that men and women participate in peace work.
3. In the large group, ask each small group to report their findings.

II. Divide the large group into small groups of women-only and men-only.
1. Ask each group to share successes and challenges in working with the opposite sex on peace issues. Challenge the groups to provide as many real examples as possible, both positive and negative.
2. Ask each group to discuss strategies for working with the opposite sex on peace issues.

- Have each group report back their findings and strategies.
- In mixed pairs of one woman and one man, ask participants to respond to each other about the reports. Each person should take a turn talking about his or her feelings about the dialogue while the other listens and tries to understand, not interrupting.

✱ *This exercise was adapted from the Women in Peacebuilding Resource and Training Manual, edited by Lisa Schirch. The full manual can be found at http://www.iiav.nl/epublications/2004/womens_peacebuilding _manual.pdf or at http://www.ifor.org/WPP/resources.htm*

10/10 STRATEGIES

Time: 30 minutes or longer
Goal or purpose of the exercise: To help people learn about the rich history of nonviolent campaigns and to gain a better understanding of campaigns, tactics, and movements.

How it's done/facilitator's notes

Ask people to break into small groups of five to six people (groups should be of equal numbers). Ask one person in each group to list the numbers 1 to 10 on a piece of paper. Tell the groups they are 'competing' with one another to see who can do the task fastest (as opposed to our usual cooperative style). Tell each group to list 10 wars as quickly as possible, raising their hands when they are done. Quietly note the time. Then ask them to list 10 nonviolent campaigns and again raise their hands when done. Note how it likely takes longer to list nonviolent campaigns than wars (although we will not discuss this point further here).

Starting with the 'winning' group, write a list of nonviolent campaigns on a wall chart. Ask other groups to add to the list. There will probably be a mix of movements, tactics, campaigns, etc. List them all; use the list to explain the differences so that participants can learn about strategic processes and how effective strategies develop. For example, the list may include 'anti-apartheid' (a movement),'Salt March' (a campaign), and 'sit-ins' (a tactic). Using the list, ask the participants to describe components of campaigns, identify tactics, and describe what makes a movement. Use a well-known campaign as a case study to learn about the strategic development of non-violent campaigns. You can also use this list to introduce people to campaigns with which they are not familiar. This list can become the basis of a longer discussion. Adjust the time according the group's needs and knowledge.

THE TREE

Time: Minimum 30 minutes
Goal or purpose of the exercise: To identify and analyse the nature and components of a problem and to come up with positive responses.

How it's done/facilitator's notes

Draw a tree with roots, a trunk, and branches with fruit. The tree represents the problem you will analyse. Ask participants to identify the roots (causes), the fruits (consequences), and the trunk (the institutions that uphold the system.) You can also add underlying principles found in the soil that 'nurture' these root causes.

Healthy Tree

What is the healthy fruit we want to grow? What roots do we need in order to grow healthy fruit? What roots do we need to cut? What structures need to be developed for a healthy society? What needs to be resisted? What values need to be in the soil to strengthen the roots? Identify goals for growing a healthy tree or goals for cutting down an unhealthy tree. Can we answer the above questions positively?

Analyse the Problem Tree

Choose the institution in the trunk of the tree that your group wants to weaken. Draw another tree, identifying the root causes and consequences. Use the list of questions above to analyse the situation or use the questions on p34.

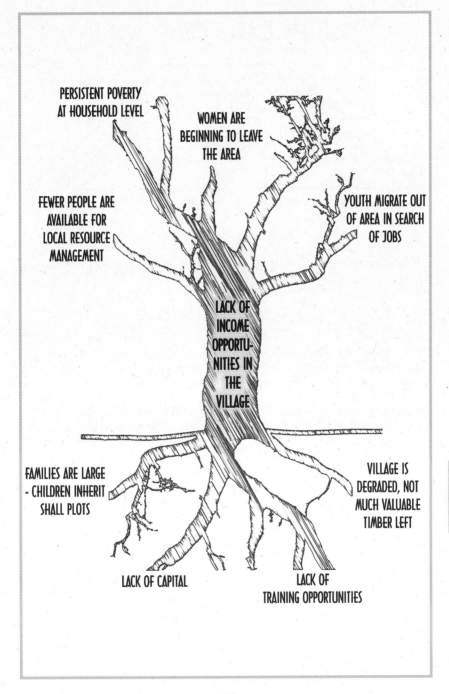

PERSISTENT POVERTY
AT HOUSEHOLD LEVEL

WOMEN ARE
BEGINNING TO LEAVE
THE AREA

FEWER PEOPLE ARE
AVAILABLE FOR
LOCAL RESOURCE
MANAGEMENT

YOUTH MIGRATE OUT
OF AREA IN SEARCH
OF JOBS

LACK OF
INCOME
OPPORTU-
NITIES IN
THE
VILLAGE

FAMILIES ARE LARGE
- CHILDREN INHERIT
SHALL PLOTS

VILLAGE IS
DEGRADED, NOT
MUCH VALUABLE
TIMBER LEFT

LACK OF CAPITAL

LACK OF
TRAINING OPPORTUNITIES

THE PILLARS OF POWER

Refusal of work contracts for immigrants (Mexican chicanos)

Fear and passivity of the Chicanos
Dominating power: firms, owners
Local political forces
Media
Silence of churches
Armed forces
Passivity of middle class and intellectuals
Passivity of workers
International economic interests

Time: Minimum 30 minutes

Goal or purpose of the exercise:
- To identify the pillars holding up the power structures we want to over come.
- To analyse the pillars with the goal of developing strategies to weaken them.
- To identify the vulnerability of power structures.

How it's done/facilitator's notes

Describe the Pillars

1. Draw an upside down triangle with pillars holding it up. Write the name of the problem in the triangle. It can be an institution or an injustice (e.g., 'war').
2. Ask the group to identify the pillars that represent the institutions and factors that support the problem (e.g., the military, corporations, patriotic citizens). Be specific about elements of the support structures (e.g., the military includes the leadership, soldiers, veterans, military families). This will help as we analyse how to weaken the structure.
3. Identify the underlying principles that are the foundation of the pillars (e.g., sexism, greed, lies).

Analyse a Pillar

Choose a pillar that your group wants to knock down. Consider your group's mission as you make your decision. Draw another set of pillars, writing the name of the institution from your chosen pillar in the triangle. Now analyse what holds up that problem. This can become the basis for developing your strategy.

Explain to the group that while the problem seems hard to shake, the inverted triangle symbolises its weakness. Whole pillars do not need to be knocked down to weaken power; weakening the pillars can have a great effect.

CONSEQUENCES OF FEAR

Time: Minimum 1 hour
Goal or purpose of the exercise: To share and analyse the causes and consequences of fear.

How it's done/facilitator's notes

Ask the members of the group to refer to an experience when they felt fear. Divide into small groups so that everyone can participate. One person should take notes about the consequences of fear. Afterwards, in a large group, write up the central ideas on the wall. Another option is to ask people to draw a situation when they felt fear. Discuss the drawing, focusing on the subjective experience (what participants thought, felt, what happened in the body, what reactions were, etc.), not simply re-constructing the facts.

It is important to end the exercise discussing the value of various alternatives that we can use against fear, to end on the positive. The exercise aims to help people to share experiences, identify their reactions, and know better how to deal with problems.

Exercises

SPECTRUM OF ALLIES

Time: Minimum 20 minutes
Goal or purpose of the exercise:
■ To understand who our allies and opponents are.
■ To help in realising that tactics need to be planned in relation to how much they do or do not attract key allies and move people towards being active allies.
■ To encourage more optimistic mobilisation efforts through realising it is not necessary to win over the opposition to our point of view.
■ To invite people into the fascinating complexity of strategising.

How it's done/facilitator's notes

This exercise uses a newsprint diagram to explore the idea that most social change situations involve a struggle between those who want the change and those who don't. Represent those who want the change by a point at one side of the sheet (say, on the left) and the opponents by a point at the other side. Explain that societies (or towns or states) usually include a range of groups that can be put on a spectrum from closest to the point of view of the advocates to farthest away. Draw a horizontal line representing this spectrum. Draw a half-moon or half a pie with wedges (as on the diagram below). The wedges closest to either end represent active allies and opponents, the next passive allies and opponents, and the group in the middle neutral parties.

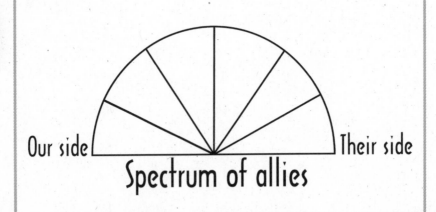

Our side — Their side
Spectrum of allies

Use the issue you are working on; if this is a general training, ask for an example of an issue that people in the group might be working on or interested in. State a demand related to the issue. Ask who in society might be inclined to be most supportive, least supportive, and in the middle. Give examples: 'unions', 'poor people's groups', 'Chamber of Commerce', etc. As participants identify groups and their locations on the spectrum, write them into the 'pie'. Identify why people are neutral; discuss if there are ways to move them toward becoming allies. Also note where people may already have moved from one wedge to another and discuss why (e.g., soldiers and veterans tend to support wars in the beginning, but as the war wages, opposition develops).

Give the good news: in most social change campaigns, it is not necessary to win the opponent to your point of view, even if the powerholders are the opponent. It is only necessary to move some or all of the pie wedges one step in your direction. If we shift each wedge one step, we are likely to win, even though the hardliners on the other side don't budge.

As the group develops its strategy and its tactics, it needs to identify which wedge it wants to address and how it can move people. In making choices about whom to reach out to, ask questions such as: which groups do we have some access to or credibility with? Which groups are not being reached? Given our group's purpose, which groups are we most suited to persuade?

This exercise can be done in as little as 20 minutes, but you can spend much more time filling in the wedges and analysing the situation.

✱ *Taken from: http://www.trainingforchange.org/content/view/69/39*

TREE AND WIND TRUST GAME

Time: 30 minutes
Goal or purpose of the exercise: To highlight situations of insecurity or fear and to gain confidence in yourself and the group.

How it's done/facilitator's notes

Form a tight circle of six to seven people, with one person in the middle. Ask the person in middle to place his/her feet solidly on the ground, close his/her eyes, and let him/herself fall to one side (as if a tree being moved by the wind). Ask the rest of the group to keep their hands in front of their bodies and pass the person in the middle from one to the other, without any brusque movement, not letting the person fall. It's important that all in the circle coordinate to make the 'tree' move from one side to the other. After a minute, ask another person from the group to go to the middle. It's important that all people participate, so that they can share their experiences.

Once each person has had a turn in the middle, on a big sheet of paper, write the feelings and experiences that everyone had during the game. Relate these impressions to fear. Compare some real situations where fear appears or some consequences of it with what the group has said. Summarise the consequences of fear and what can be done to overcome it.

DECISION-MAKING

Time: Minimum 30 minutes

Goal or purpose of the exercise: To prepare people to face crisis situations and to develop a frame of mind of thinking quickly under stress, focusing on key issues while learning to ignore minor ones, so as to reach action-decisions.

How it's done/facilitator's notes

To a group no larger than eight people (this can be a small group, with others observing), give a scenario. For example: 'A woman faints inside the line of a march. You are a peacekeeper. What do you do'? Allow 15 seconds for discussion among the three or four people taking part. Afterwards, discuss with all participants. Ask: How did you come to a decision? What helped the process? What was the main difficulty?

Another step is to practice the exercise with a spokescouncil. Form several small groups that act as 'affinity groups'. Give them a new scenario, and ask each group to choose a spokesperson. Once each 'affinity group' has come to a decision, have the different spokespersons meet to come to a decision. After they reach a level of consensus, ask each spokesperson to consult with their 'affinity group' about the spokescouncil's decision. Each group can make recommendations for changes if necessary. Then have the spokescouncil meet again to come to a final decision that hopefully will be a decision that everyone in all of the 'affinity groups' can live with.

Please note that a major limitation is that doing too many quick decision exercises, especially right before an action takes place, can establish a mind-set of emergency, thus raising tension so that people panic. Quick decision exercises should be tempered with other training experiences to prevent this perspective of imminent danger.

Exercises

ROLE PLAYING

Time: Minimum 20 minutes

Goal or purpose of the exercise: Role playing is a simulation exercise in which participants take on roles in a given situation as preparation for encountering a similar situation or evaluating a past one. Role playing is used to develop a sense of tactics, individual competence, and group cohesion. The main advantage of role playing over other tools is that by its nature it involves people's emotions as well as their intellects in the experience. Because participants are more deeply engaged in role playing than they are in discussing a situation, they learn more and probably more quickly. Role plays are a versatile tool that can be used for many different purposes, for example: to analyse situations, theories and tactics; to understand people and their roles; to develop insight into the thoughts and feelings of one's 'opponents'; to anticipate new situations; to reveal fears, anxieties, and other feelings people have about an action; to develop individual and group competence and confidence; and to develop group morale.

How it's done/facilitator's notes

Although role plays can be very complicated and involve many participants, they often are designed to look at a limited situation and not an entire action. Consider what the group needs to practise to prepare for an action. (See 'Roles Before, During, and After an Action', p86, to determine roles that may be needed.)

Set the scene, often with a few very simple items to prepare the scene and characterise the roles, so that all participants understand the physical setting in which the role play will take place. Give the participants a description of their role, especially including the motives and interests of the role, rather than a screen play to act out. Give people a few minutes to get into their role, and, if they are in a group, possibly to map out tactics. Be clear when the role play begins and when it ends. Ask role players to start at the given scene and play their role as they see it.

It is best to end the role play as soon as enough important issues are uncovered. It is important for the trainer(s) to act to prevent physical or emotional injury to the participants, possibly by quickly stopping the role play if situations that endanger the participants develop.

After stopping the role play, give the participants a brief pause to lay down their roles. Then begin an evaluation. This is an essential part of the role play exercise. It is often advantageous to begin with allowing the participants to share the emotions that came up during the role play. If not everyone could see the entire role play, it helps to have a very brief overview of the events. Participants can share what they learned during the exercise. Observers can share their views about what happened, what went well, what needs improvement, what precipitated increased or decreased tension, etc.

Set the tone for the evaluation, helping the group members to share their feelings or tensions and what they learned or observed about tactics, strategy, goals, nonviolence theory, and its application. Discourage evaluating how 'well' the participants played a role. There is no one 'right' answer to a given situation so it is important to help the group to express its ideas and alternative solutions for that situation. For a short role play, usually twenty minutes is enough. It is often helpful to start another role play that can allow the group to try alternatives that came up in the evaluation rather than continue the discussion. One way to do this is to repeat the same basic plot with different people in the roles or change the situation by bringing in new roles, such as police or crowd reactions.

An evaluation should only go on as long as new issues are raised and participants are exploring problems and alternatives.

CROSS SPECTRUM

Time: Minimum 20 minutes
Goal or purpose of the exercise:
■ To help a group determine what an effective nonviolent action is.
■ To show different perceptions on nonviolence
■ To test or develop a specific proposal for effective nonviolent action on which the group agrees.

How it's done/facilitator's notes

Make a large cross (+) on the floor with masking tape, long enough to make a grid on which the group members can stand. Write 'nonviolent' and 'violent' on opposite ends of one line and 'effective' and 'not effective' on opposite ends of the other. (Instead of tape, you can simply put the words on paper at ends of four sides.) Present a possible action scenario; ask people to stand in a place on the grid that represents how they feel about it (e.g., nonviolent but not effective). Ask some of the people to explain why they are standing where they are. Let people know that if they are 'moved' by what is said, they can change positions.

If the purpose of this exercise is to create an effective nonviolent action for a certain situation, use scenario suggestions that move people towards the nonviolent and effective corner. As you discuss, make a list of what people identify as needed to make the action more effective and nonviolent (e.g., training all the participants, good media work, etc.) If the purpose is to show different perceptions on nonviolence, suggest a wide variety of scenarios (both from you and from the participants themselves).

Ask questions to get the group thinking more deeply about what is effective and nonviolent. Depending on the purpose of the exercise, this exercise can be done in as little as 20 minutes to show how people feel about actions; it can be extended until a satisfactory nonviolent action scenario is developed if that is the goal. This is also a good exercise to use in conjunction with brainstorming.

FORUM THEATRE

Time: Minimum 45 minutes
Goal or purpose of the exercise: To explore different scenarios and options; to develop new alternatives.

How it's done/facilitator's notes

Forum Theatre is a form of role playing that can be used for public action (see 'Turkey: Building a Nonviolent Culture', p104). The basic idea is to act out a scenario, perhaps leading to an undesirable conclusion or violence and then to begin acting out the scenario again. This time, however, either a participant in the role play or any observer can shout 'freeze' and take over a role in the scenario to try to do something differently.

A short example of forum theatre

Plot: Two members of your group visit a state official to report an act of violence against your group. It is unclear whether the police and whoever attacked your group collaborated. Before entering the official's office, ask the group members to decide what documentation about the attack they have as well as what they want to achieve. Ask the person playing the official to take a certain attitude (ranging from generally sympathetic to feigning that s/he will take it seriously to downright hostility and counter-attacking) and motive (such as a desire to keep group quiet or to find out as much about them as possible). Ask the official to begin the meeting with something somewhat disruptive, such as taking the initiative him/herself (or at least telling them how busy s/he is and perhaps asking to see their identity cards). S/he should also consider doing something friendly or scary (friendly would be reminiscing about his or her activist youth or claiming friendship with parents of some group members; frightening would be showing knowledge of private lives of group members).
Cast: 2-4 group members, 1 official, 1 official's receptionist
Role play: Play out the scenario once through. When the group replays, ask the official to introduce new challenges for the group. Remind people that if they have a new idea to try, call out 'freeze' and take the place of one of the group members.
Discussion points: What were reasonable objectives for the group members? How could they take the initiative in the situation? How much did they want to divulge about the group and its members? Were they putting other group members or their families at risk? If they convinced the official to promise to do something, how could they firm that into an agreement and make sure it happens? How could they have prepared better for this visit?

TOOLS FOR GROUNDING, PROTECTING, AND BLOCKADING

Time: 10 minutes for each
Goal or purpose of the exercise: To learn tools that can help you protect yourself and others in your group and de-escalate a situation.

How it's done/facilitator's note

■ Centring: When you are centred, you are calm, stable, present in the moment, and hard to push off balance physically or emotionally. You can also have a calming effect on those around you. In order to centre yourself, focus on your centre of gravity. It's just below your navel, deep inside your body. Focus here when you feel upset or under pressure in order to ground yourself and reconnect with your power within.

■ Point to attacker: You can make a violent attack very visible by getting everyone in the vicinity to sit down so the attacker is suddenly visible to all and to the media.

■ Puppy pile: To protect someone being attacked on the ground. One person kneels and forms a bridge with their body over the victim; others then pile onto the bridge. Don't squash the person attacked!

■ Step in between perpetrator and demonstrator: Keep your palms open and visible, try not to touch the attacker, or at the very least, do not hold onto him or her. Just inter-positioning yourself can often be enough to stop an attack. Talk reassuringly to the attacker.

■ Surround ("U') and move perpetrator away: With several people, step between the attacker and the demonstrator, form a U shape around the perpetrator, and move him or her away. Don't completely surround the attacker; make sure to leave him or her an 'out'. Talk with the attacker reassuringly as you do this.

■ Surround ("O') and absorb demonstrator: Totally surround a demonstrator who's being attacked and absorb him or her back into the crowd.

■ Form a line between opposing factions/blocking: Knees relaxed and not locked, stand shoulder-width apart. Be aware of how strong a line you need to make and the different impacts of different stances, e.g.: standing separately > holding hands > linking elbows > linking wrists.

■ Staying put/holding your ground: For use, for example, in a blockade. Centre yourself, send your roots down deep into the earth, feel yourself relaxed and heavy.

Other variations

■ Sitting in a row: place larger people on the ends.

■ Sitting in a circle: Cross your hands between your legs and hold each others' wrists with a strong grip. In this formation, you can see each other and give emotional support. Make sure to warn each other about what's happening behind, where the other side of the circle cannot see.

■ Sitting in a column: Wrap your legs round the person in front, lean forward, put your hands around the chest of the person in front of you, and keep your head down.

■ Self-defence posture: First lace your hands together at the base of your skull, with your elbows together protecting your temples. Curl up in a foetal position on the ground, lying on your right side to protect your liver. Most main organs and head are thus protected, although your kidneys are still vulnerable

SPECTRUM/BAROMETER

Time: 10 minutes per statement; more if needed, less if there is clear agreement.

Goal or purpose of the exercise: To see and hear the spectrum of people's thoughts on an issue and to take a barometer reading of where a group stands on a statement.

How it's done/facilitator's notes

Identify a space where group members can place themselves along a line. One end of the spectrum represents 'agreement', the other end 'disagreement' (these words can be posted at each end as a reminder). Present a clear statement (one idea, not more than a sentence or two), and ask people to stand in a place on the spectrum that represents how they feel about it. Make it clear that there are no 'right' or 'wrong' answers, just different opinions, and that it is important to listen to each other and try to understand each others' perspectives. Ask some people to explain why they are standing where they are; explain that people can be 'moved' by what they hear. Allow time for discussion.

If agreement is needed (e.g., for Nonviolence Guidelines) and there is wide range of disagreement, ask a few people from either end of the spectrum to get together and and see if they can rewrite the statement in hopes of reaching agreement.

Examples of statements

■ Individual Principles of Nonviolent Action (see p31.)
■ Individual Nonviolence Guidelines (see p32)

9

DO IT YOURSELF: CREATING A HANDBOOK

Since this is an international Handbook, we realise that many groups will translate materials to create their own handbooks. If you are thinking of producing your own handbook, here are some tips. First, you need to be clear about your goals and the amount of energy you are willing to put into a handbook (see questions below under goals and content). Another important aspect is thinking about what would make your handbook special.

Here is a list of questions that may be useful before starting your own handbook project:

Goals

- What is the main reason for the handbook?
- Who is the handbook for?
- How do you want the handbook to be used?
- What do you need to include in the handbook?
- Have you checked existing handbooks? What don't you like about them or find not useful?

Content

- What topics and themes do you want include?
- How do you want to structure the handbook?
- How long will your handbook be?
- Will you use only new texts or existing ones?
- Who will choose existing texts and write new ones?
- What is the timeline for this work?
- How should the handbook be used? Can people just read a section that is relevant or do they need to read the full handbook?

Production

- How would you fund the handbook?
- Do you want to sell it or give it out for free?
- What will the distribution scope be?
- What kind of layout do you want (e.g., paper size, graphic styles)?
- How will you evaluate the handbook?

DIY

INDEPENDENCE DAY DEMONSTRATION, BOGOTÁ, COLOMBIA.
PHOTO: COLLECTIVE ACTION OF CONSCIENTIOUS OBJECTORS IN BOGOTÁ

10

GLOSSARY OF TERMS

Affinity group
Autonomous group of 5 to 15 persons in which group members not only have an affinity for each other, but know each other's strengths and weaknesses and support each other as they participate (or intend to participate) in a nonviolent campaign together. This group makes decisions about the action together.

Boycott
Social, economic, or political non-cooperation.

Bustcard
Pocket guideline with recommendations on what to do if stopped by the police during an action.

Campaign
A series of activities and actions done over a period of time to achieve specific, stated goals. Campaigns are started by a group of people with a common understanding and vision who identify goals and begin a process of research, education, and training that will strengthen and grow the number of participants who engage in the activities and actions.

Civil disobedience
The active refusal to obey certain laws, demands, or commands of a government or of an occupying power without resorting to physical violence. It is one of the primary tactics of nonviolent resistance.

Conflict resolution
Reconciling opposing perspectives, stories, or experiences and deciding on a response that promotes and protects the human rights of all parties concerned.

Consensus decision-making
A decision-making process that aims to take everyone's concerns into consideration, often modifying a proposed solution several times in the process. It is based on listening, respect, and participation by everyone. Consensus decision-making differs greatly from majority decision-making, which often leads to a power struggle between two different solutions.

Constructive programme
The process of building a new society in the shell of the old. As Robert Burrowes describes it: 'For the individual, constructive programme meant increased power-from-within through the development of personal identity, self-reliance, and fearlessness. For the community, it meant the creation of a new set of political, social, and economic relations'. In cases where political revolutions have taken place but

the population was not organised to exercise self-determination, creating a new society has been extremely difficult, and a new dictatorship usurping power has too often been the result.

■ Debriefing
A process after an action or a training experience in which group members share what they experienced, felt, and learnt during the experiencing, as well as look at how these learnings may be helpful in the future.

■ Direct action
Any action where individuals or groups act directly themselves to try to bring about change rather than asking or expecting others to act on their behalf. Interrupting a pro-nuclear sermon in church would be direct action; writing to a vicar's bishop to complain about the sermon would be indirect action. Either could be an effective way of raising the issue.

■ Empowerment
Supporting people to have more control over their own lives. Empowerment can involve gaining skills (or having one's own skills and knowledge), increasing self-confidence, and developing self-reliance.

■ Facilitation
Is used in a variety of group settings to describe the action of a person (facilitator) whose role is to work with group processes to ensure that meetings run well and achieve a high degree of consensus, to help a group of people understand their common objectives, and to assist them to plan to achieve those objectives. This is done without the facilitator taking a particular position in the discussion.

■ Gender
Gender is a social construction of ideas that defines the roles, belief systems and attitudes, images, values, and expectations of men and women. It contributes heavily to power relationships, not only between men and women, but also within each group. This results in many social problems.

■ Human rights
Legal rights guaranteeing every human being's life, liberty, and security of person, based on international treaties and law.

■ Nonviolence
Either (1) The behaviour of people who in a conflict refrain from violent acts; or (2) Any of several belief systems that reject violence (both physical and structural) on principle, not just as impractical. Otherwise, the term is best not used, since it often contributes to ambiguity and confusion. To describe specific actions or movements, the recommended terms are: 'nonviolent action', 'nonviolent resistance', or 'nonviolent struggle'.

■ Nonviolent action
An action based on the desire to end violence — be that physical violence or what's been called "structural violence" of deprivation, social exclusion and oppression — without committing further violence. It is an alternative to both passive submission and violence. The techniques used in nonviolent action include many specific methods, which are grouped into three main classes: nonviolent protest and persuasion, non-cooperation, and nonviolent intervention.

Nonviolent resistance

Nonviolent struggle, conducted largely by non-cooperation, in reaction to an act, policy, or government a person or group disapproves of. The broader terms 'nonviolent action' and 'nonviolent struggle' are preferred to refer to the overall nonviolent technique of action and to action in which a nonviolent group also takes the initiative or intervenes, as in a sit-in.

Nonviolent struggle

A synonym for 'nonviolent action'. This term may be used also to indicate that the nonviolent action in a conflict is particularly purposeful or aggressive. 'Nonviolent struggle' is especially useful to describe nonviolent action against determined and resourceful opponents who use repressive measures and countermeasures.

Pacifism

Opposition to war or violence as a means of settling disputes or gaining advantage. Pacifism covers a spectrum of views ranging from believing that international disputes can and should be peacefully resolved; to calls for abolishing the institutions of the military and war; to opposing any organisation of society through governmental force (anarchist or libertarian pacifism); to rejecting the use of physical violence to obtain political, economic, or social goals; to condemning force except in cases where it is absolutely necessary to advance the cause of peace (pacifism); to opposing violence under any circumstance, including defence of self and others.

People power

The power capacity of a mobilised population and its institutions using nonviolent forms of struggle. The term was especially used during the 1986 Philippine nonviolent insurrection.

Power

Can be defined as the ability to have an impact on the world. Power may be seen in different forms:
- Power with: power that comes from people acting in cooperation. Individually, they may be powerless, but together they are greater than the sum of their parts.
- Power to: an enabling power, derived from an inner conviction, acquired knowledge, or skill, an investment of trust or assistance from others, or from the ability to use external resources (e.g., money, tools).
- Power over: the power of dominance in which the will of one person or group prevails.

Snatch squad

A police riot control tactic in which several officers, usually in protective riot gear, rush forwards, sometimes in a flying wedge formation to break through the front of the crowd and to snatch one or more individuals from a demonstration.

Social movements

A type of group action. They are large, informal groupings of individuals and/or organisations focused on specific political or social issues, in other words, on carrying out, resisting, or undoing a social change.

Strategy and tactic

Terms that are often confused. Tactics are the actual means used to gain an objective, while strategy is

145

the overall campaign plan, which may involve complex operational patterns, activity, and decision-making that lead to tactical execution. Strategy is a long-term plan of action designed to achieve a particular goal, most often 'winning'. Strategy is differentiated from a tactic or immediate actions with resources at hand because it is extensively premeditated and often practically rehearsed. Strategies are used to make the problem or problems easier to understand and solve.

■ Violence

Inflicting or threatening to inflict physical injury or death on people. All behaviour cannot be neatly classified as either 'violence' or 'nonviolence'; several categories fall between these two extremes, including 'destruction of property'. In reporting on a demonstration or resistance movement which is primarily or exclusively non-violent, care is required to distinguish it, for example, from the acts of violence by small numbers of persons (who may be undisciplined or deliberately disruptive for political reasons or as agents provocateurs). Similarly, a demonstration should not be described as 'violent' when it is violently attacked by police or troops but nevertheless maintains its nonviolent discipline.

11

RESOURCES

Other Training Manuals and Web Resources on Nonviolence

■ *Resource Manual for a Living Revolution*, Virginia Coover, Ellen Deacon, Charles Esser, and Christopher Moore (New Society Publishers; first edition 1977, latest 1985; 351 pages). Familiarly known as the 'Monster Manual', this was the comprehensive sourcebook for English-speaking nonviolence trainers in the 1970s and 1980s, produced collectively within the United States by Movement for a New Society.

■ *Nonviolent Action Handbook*, Beck, Sanderson, Goleta, (World Peace Communications; 2002; 95 pages). Introductory texts, downloadable or as print copies from World Peace Communications, 495 Whitman St. #A, Goleta, CA 93117, USA. http://san.beck.org/NAH1-Nonviolence.html

■ *Nonviolence Trainers Resource Manual* (Nonviolence Training Project; May 1995; 211 pages). Wide-ranging manual with sections on defining nonviolence, power and conflict, learning from other movements, strategic frameworks, non-violence and communication, working in groups, and preparing for nonviolent action. PDF download at: http://www.nonviolence.org.au/downloads/trainers_resource_manual_may05.pdf

■ *The Ruckus Society Website* offers manuals on action planning and media among other topics, plus numerous links to other Websites: see http://www.ruckus.org/

■ *Handbook for Nonviolent Action* (War Resisters League, Donnelly/Colt Graphix; 1989; 36 pages). Designed as a tool for learning about different aspects of nonviolent civil disobedience actions. Most of it can be downloaded as part of ACT UP New York's *Manual for Civil Disobedience*: see http://www.actupny.org/documents/CDdocuments/CDindex.html

■ *Seeds for Change:* A British-based network that provides training resources including: consensus and facilitation, groups and meetings, practical skills for campaigning groups: see http://seedsforchange.org.uk/free/resources

■ *Rant Collective:* A trainers' collective that offers resources on action planning & structures, anti-oppression, media, and strategy: see http://www.rantcollective.net/article.php?list=type&type=17

Nonviolent Action (General)

■ *The Albert Einstein Institute*: nonviolent action, frequently asked questions about nonviolent action, 198 methods of nonviolent action, applications of non-violent action, case studies, publications on nonviolent action in many languages: see http://www.aeinstein.org

■ *The Politics of Nonviolent Action*, Gene Sharp (Porter Sargent; 1973; 3 volumes). Now classic analysis of the theory and dynamics of nonviolent action and an exhaustive list of methods with examples. Includes extensive bibliographical information.

■ *People Power and Protest since 1945: a bibliography on nonviolent action*, April Carter, Howard Clark, and Michael Randle (Housmans; 2006). See http://www.civilresistance.info/bibliography

Campaign Development

■ *How to Win Campaigns: 100 Steps to Success*, Chris Rose (Earthscan; 2005).

■ *The Strategy of Nonviolent Defense*, Robert J. Burrowes (State University of New York Press; 1996).

■ *Justice Ignited: The Dynamics of Backfire*, Brian Martin (Rowman & Littlefield; 2007).

■ *Doing Democracy: The MAP Model for Organizing Social Movements*, Bill Moyer (with JoAnn McAllister, Mary Lou Finley, and Steven Soifer), (New Society Publishers; 2001; 228 pages). Includes Movement Action Plan - a tool of strategic analysis for nonviolent movements. For resources on the Movement Action Plan, see http://www.turning-the-tide.org/files/Bill%20Moyer%208-stages%20Social%20Movements%20Hand-out.pdf

Direct Action

■ *DIY or Die*: Website with links to different resources for nonviolent direct action: see http://www.sprayism.com/dawiki/doku.php?id=guides

■ *The activist tool box*: Nonviolence direct action tool box: see http://www.uhc-collective.org.uk/webpages/toolbox/index.htm

■ *Peace News tools section*: Collection of different resources in nonviolence from practical tools to nonviolence analysis: see http://peacenews.info/tools/index.php

■ *Starhawk's Resources for Activism Trainers*: Resources for nonviolent direct action and anti-oppression trainers/preparers, magical activism workshop facilitators, and consensus decision making: see http://www.starhawk.org/activism/trainer-resources/trainer-resources.htm

Organisational Structures/Facilitation

■ *The Tyranny of Structurelessness*, Jo Freeman (1970). An analysis of why 'structurelessness' does not work if we want to be effective: http://flag.blackened.net/revolt/hist_texts/structurelessness.html
■ *Meeting Facilitation — The No-Magic Method*, Berit Lakey. How to develop good group structures, with resources on: agenda planning, facilitation, and roles in a group: see http://www.reclaiming.org/resources/consensus/blakey.htm

Decision-Making (including Consensus)

■ *Papers on Nonviolent Action and Cooperative Decision-Making*, Randy Schutt. A nonviolence trainer's sample agendas and workshop notes dealing with preparing for nonviolent action, nonviolent action strategic planning, cooperative decision-making, and interpersonal behaviour:
see http://www.vernalproject.org/RPapers/html
■ *INNATE: Irish Network for Nonviolent Action Training & Education*. Consensus for Small Groups: an introduction and worksheets. More resources on nonviolence training available at http://www.innatenonviolence.org/workshops/consensussmallgroups.shtml

Dealing with Emotions and Trauma (Fear, Burn-Out, Anger)

Both of these websites have resources in many languages and links to other good resources.
■ *Activist Trauma Support:* This Website is primarily for political activists who may be injured during or by their political activities and/or who are struggling with other mental health issues related to activism. Resources are available in many different languages: see http://www.activist-trauma.net
■ *T-team:* a collective of activists in Tel Aviv, historical Palestine, who've come together to support activists going through intense emotional (and post-traumatic) experiences as a result of their work:
see http://the-t-team.blogspot.com/

Anti-Oppression

Each of these resources is deeply connected to a particular country and cultural context, but as examples, they can provide ideas and inspiration for people everywhere.

■ *Training for Change, USA*. Resources on diversity and anti-oppression. See http://www.trainingforchange.org/content/category/4/28/56/index.html
■ *Uprooting Racism: How White People Can Work for Racial Justice*, Paul Kivel (New Society Publishers; 2002). A book written for white activists working against racism within the United States.

■ *Confronting Racism in Communities: Guidelines and Resources for Anti-Racism Training Resources*, David Hollinsworth. A training manual produced for groups addressing racism in Australia. The document is available as a pdf on the Web from the Change Agency Education and Training Institute: see http://www.thechangeagency.org/_dbase_upl/Anti-Racism%20Training.pdf

■ *Henry Martyn Institute, India:* Henry Martyn Institute in Hyderabad, India, established itself as a an ecumenical Christian organisation, dedicated to the objective study and teaching of Islam and the promotion of interfaith dialogue. In recent years, however, its work has expanded to include a praxis program and training for communities in addressing religious and various identity-based conflicts in Indian communities.
Contact: Henry Martyn Institute, 6-3-128/1, Beside National Police Academy, Shivarampally, Hyderabad — 500 0520 India
E-mail: hyd1_hmiis@sancharnet.in Web: http://www.hmiindia.com/index.htm
Praxis Program: see http://www.hmiindia.com/praxis_crVision.htm

■ *Soulforce:* an organisation committed to using nonviolence to end violence against gays, lesbians, bi-sexuals and transgendered people (LGBT) in the United States. The mission of Soulforce is to cut off homophobia at its source: religious bigotry. It applies the creative direct action principles taught by Gandhi and Martin Luther King Jr. to peacefully resist injustice and demand full equality for LGBT citizens and same-gender families. Their Website includes videos, articles, handouts, and action campaign ideas: see http://www.soulforce.org/index.php

Gender Awareness

■ *Women's International League for Peace and Freedom:* see http://www.peacewomen.org. Includes women's peace and security resources, with materials from many cultures and contexts and a number of handbooks and training resources.
See also http://www.peacewomen.org/resources/Organizing/organizingindex.html

■ *The Inclusive Security Sustainable Peace: A Toolkit for Advocacy and Action.* Developed by International Alert and Women Waging Peace, available in PDF format at: http:// www.womenbuildingpeace.org
or http://www.womenwagingpeace.net

■ *Advocacy Guide for Feminists:* see http://www.awid.org/eng/Issues-and-Analysis/Library/An-advocacy-guide-for-feminists

■ *Claiming Justice, Claiming Rights: A Guide for Women Human Rights Defenders*, see http://www.defendingwomen-defendingrights.org/pdf2007/book3Neo.pdf

■ *International Women's Partnership for Peace and Justice:* see http://www.womenforpeaceandjustice.org/

■ *Women Peacemakers Program:* see http://www.ifor.org/WPP/index.html

■ *Women in Black:* see http://www.womeninblack.org/

Working with Media

- http://www.communitybuilders.nsw.gov.au/getting_organised/message/media1.html
- http://www.octobertech.com/october/handbook.nsf/pages/Media
- http://www.unicef.org/righttoknow/index_mediacampaign.html
- http://www.bbc.co.uk/dna/actionnetwork/A4288908
- http://www.ruckus.org/article.php?list=type&type=18

Online media centres/contact examples:
- http://www.jubileedebtcampaign.org.uk/media
- http://www.greenpeace.org/international/press/